The Self-Hypnosis
Solution

*Step-by-Step Methods and Scripts to Create
Profound Change and Lifelong Results*

By
Dr. Richard Nongard
America's #1 Leading Self-Hypnosis Expert

Subliminal Science Press
Las Vegas, Nevada

The Self-Hypnosis Solution: *Step-by-Step Methods and Scripts to Create Profound Change and Lifelong Results*

ISBN: 978-1-7344678-4-0
Dr. Richard K. Nongard

First Printing: August 2020
Imprint: Subliminal Science Press
Dr. Richard K. Nongard
Hypnosis Nevada, LLC
15560 N. Frank L. Wright Blvd. B4-118
Scottsdale, AZ 85260
(702) 418-3332

www.NongardBooks.com

www.SelfHypnosisSolution.com

Dr. Richard Nongard is available to speak at your business or conference event on a variety of topics. Call (702) 418-3332 for booking information.

Why Read This Book?

This book teaches you the easy to follow methods of self-hypnosis that Dr. Richard Nongard has taught countless others over his 30 years as a professional hypnotist.

What are your intentions? Do you intend to make lasting changes in your relationships, habits, behaviors, or attitudes? To be successful, you will need a blueprint to take you from your intentions to actions that drive unlimited success. This book is that blueprint. With self-hypnosis scripts, step-by-step techniques for change, and precise instructions, you are sure to achieve personal success in every area of life.

Like Dr. Richard Nongard's other books, this book is destined to be a preeminent book in self-hypnosis because it reveals contrasting yet highly effective strategies for creating the self-hypnosis resource state. The methods in this book will change your life by showing you the techniques and processes that will allow you to benefit from being able to hypnotize yourself fully. One method follows the traditional approach of hypnotic induction, and another is a rapid method for immediately accessing hypnotic potential. Imagine setting your intentions and benefitting from self-hypnosis from the first few pages. Additional methods revealed in these pages can be used to support and adapt these methods ot any situation or desired outcome!

This book is a recipe book that answers the question, "What am I supposed to do after I hypnotize myself?" It provides many different methods you can use to truly benefit from the proven techniques of self-hypnosis.

This book is for people who not only want to know how to do self-hypnosis but for those who want to create a more profound experience and move into a repertoire of techniques. These techniques can be easily applied to deeper states of self-hypnosis and provide lasting transformation. Learn the exact methods Dr. Nongard teaches to professional athletes, top students, business leaders, and others who come to his office because they want to move from merely learning how to solve a problem to actually living in a state of peak performance. The methods in this book can make you a better person, improve personal relationships, create wealth, put aside unwanted habits or behaviors, and live in abundance. You owe it to yourself to live your best life.

Dr. Richard Nongard is America's leading self-hypnosis expert and the author of the bestselling book *The Seven Most Effective Methods of Self-Hypnosis.* His self-hypnosis video and audio sessions have been used by hundreds of thousands of people to create lasting change, and his YouTube sessions have been viewed by millions!

Also Get the bestselling self-hypnosis book from Dr. Richard Nongard from your favorite book retailer:

The Seven Most Effective Methods of Self-Hypnosis: How to Create Rapid Change in Your Health, Your Wealth, and Your Habits

Access the free resources that accompany this book at: SelfHypnosisSolution.com

Written by a Leading Expert with 30 Years' Experience

Dr. Richard K. Nongard is an ICBCH Certified Professional Hypnotist, a Licensed Marriage and Family Therapist and an expert in helping people create lasting success. He has been a TEDx speaker, he is a popular author with over 25+ books to his credit, and his self-hypnosis videos have been seen by more than four million people.

Dr. Richard K. Nongard is the expert other professionals come to study with and learn advanced methods of professional hypnosis. In this book, he reveals the strategies that actually work and how you can do them at home. Everything is explained step-by-step. When you are finished with this book, you will have a new resource that you can tap into for the rest of your life.

Do you want Dr. Richard K. Nongard to be the motivational speaker at your next event? Call (702) 418-3332 or visit NONGARD.COM

Table of Contents

Introduction

Suspicious first-timers might ask, "Does self-hypnosis really work?" The answer: of course! Dating back centuries, various methods of self-hypnosis, meditation, autosuggestion, and self-talk have been used to create lasting, effective change. I have practiced various forms of self-hypnosis myself, and in 30 years it has helped me stop smoking, overcome anxiety, focus my attention, overcome a fear of flying, and live my dreams. In my practice as a professional hypnotist, I have witnessed tremendous change in my clients' lives, funneled by self-hypnosis training and coaching. Some of my clients have seized control of lifelong battles with depression or anger, other clients have rapidly lost weight, and many more have developed confidence, set intentions, and created wealth—all using the principles of self-hypnosis.

I also train corporate leaders and sales executives in self-hypnosis. I have seen them shift from cutting corners to reaping profits, even during economic recessions. I have helped leaders use self-hypnosis as a pathway to emotional intelligence, and I have helped people make career decisions with the clarity of mind that only self-hypnosis can provide.

The widespread advocacy of self-hypnosis stems far beyond mine and my clients' experiences; peer-reviewed academic journals extoll the profound results of self-hypnosis. The best part? The research shows expansive results: behavioral change (quitting smoking, weight loss, increase in motivation levels, etc.); emotional change (trauma recovery, overcoming depression, anxiety control, etc.); wellness change (improvement in health, surgical recovery, prevention of illness, etc.); and achieving long term success. There are even studies showing the power of self-hypnosis to enhance intimacy, sexual satisfaction, and sexual performance. Sports journals portray it is a great tool for athletes; it can enhance their endurance, their overall morale during a sports game, and increase their stamina. Educational journals suggest that it can bolster academic performance, accelerate learning, improve test-taking skills, and bring up grades.

Your mind has an incredible ability to access the resource that is a state of hypnosis and use it to help you achieve your dreams and desires! In this book I am going to guide you step-by-step through the applications of self-hypnosis. The teachings of this book are based on proven methods. This book includes worksheets to help you to gain the edge you need to step into your best life.

What do you hope to accomplish by mastering self-hypnosis? What is your hope for how it changes your behavior, your attitude, or influences your success? By mastering the contents of this book, you can experience a new sense of freedom in many areas of life, but there is probably one driving reason you bought this book.

If self-hypnosis could help you in one specific way, what would make it worth the purchase price for you? Give it some thought and then write down what you want to accomplish.

_____

_____

_____

By the time you finish this book you will have new insights for accomplishing this change. You have already taken the first step: knowing what is important to you.

I have good news for you! No matter what you wrote down, self-hypnosis is a powerful tool that will help you achieve it. Self-hypnosis is used by Olympic athletes worldwide, by titans of business and wealth creators like Napoleon Hill, and by behavioral therapists like me. Celebrities like Matt Damon and Drew Barrymore have used it to quit smoking; Sarah Ferguson, the Duchess of York, used it to lose weight.

As you move forward through this book, you will begin to discover, develop, and put into practice the incredible powers of self-hypnosis to create your best life.

~ Dr. Richard K. Nongard

The Self-Hypnosis Solution

(I have provided additional resources you can access now at my website **SelfHypnosisSolution.com** *and by accessing them now you will have them as a resource while you continue reading.)*

Chapter One: Understanding the Power of Intention

Self-hypnosis begins with your intentions. Intention drive you into success. It is the mechanism for change. There is a good chance you bought this book in order to discover a new method for finally achieving your goals. In the past, you have probably set goals and—although you hit a few of them—many were missed, forgotten, or settled for less.

Or, perhaps you are one of those people who never really sets goals. It might come from not knowing exactly how to do it, or more commonly, from mistaking dreams for goals. Dreams are the big picture ideas we have, but they are often not quantifiable. Goals can stem from dreams, but a good goal is specific and quantifiable.

Teaching people to set goals is the heart of almost every self-help book, corporate training seminar, and motivational speech. We are taught formulas for goal setting, such as S.M.A.R.T., which stands for specific, measurable, attainable, relevant, time-focused. We are taught platitudes such as, "If you aim for nothing, you will hit nothing!" and told that if we don't set goals and live a goal-directed life, we will fail at everything.

Unfortunately, the result of all this goal-setting pressure is often failure. In many cases, we miss the moment by focusing on the future, one that may never arrive as we envision it! This book contains a new method for attaining success, abundance, and lasting transformation. The idea that *by not setting goals you can wildly surpass your own expectations* is sure to be controversial, but there is a method for activating your potential that is even more powerful than goal setting:

Intention setting.

People who set goals do reach them sometimes, but goal setting can be problematic. The first issue? It keeps you focused on the problem rather than the solution—this is a huge obstacle to lasting success. Where your mind is focused is where your mind will be, and goal setting keeps us focused on what we do not yet have. Goal setting forces us to live and focus on the problem, and struggle to find solutions.

Positive Psychology is an academic discipline with evidenced-based approaches to creating lasting change. The basic premise of Positive Psychology (and its corporate counterpart,

Appreciative Inquiry) is *by staying in the problem, we rarely find a solution.*

Goals are often the product of what we believe are others' expectations of us. Sometimes in business, especially in sales, they are decided by someone else: we set goals based on our competitors' accomplishments. It causes us to look outside of ourselves and miss opportunity.

Intentions on the other hand are internal; nobody can set an intention for you. This gives you far more power.

Let's continue examining the business example to better understand the key distinctions between goal and intent:

If product returns are too high and your goal is to reduce them, then your focus is going to be on product returns rather than customer satisfaction—you end up fixating on numbers rather than people. On the other hand, you can set an intention to create loyal customers who are satisfied with their product, thereby reducing product returns. Your focus is now on the solution, not the problem. This subtle but important difference is one of the keys to success.

Let us look at goal setting in the arena of personal improvement. If your goal is weight loss, your focus is on questions such as "how fat am I still?" and "when will I no longer be obese?" Goal setting forces the mind to stay focused on the problem, creating a continual dissatisfaction over "not being there yet." This is what causes many people to downgrade their goals or completely give up on them.

The Self-Hypnosis Solution

Our natural inclination to downgrade our goals as we near the expiration date, or to allow ourselves extensions, is yet another fatal flaw of goal setting. This natural inclination can actually cause a reverse effect—a downward spiral of mediocrity as we either accept revised levels of success or extend goals into the future, rendering them meaningless and less likely to materialize. Intentions never have this flaw as intentions are meant to be attainable and pursuable immediately.

The sacrifices that goal setters make in order to reach their mark cast a large shadow on the benefits of goal keeping. In business, goal achievement often comes at the expense of professional ethics. Many large companies, including Wells Fargo and Sears, have made national news when the goals they set came at the expense of customer satisfaction. These companies might have achieved their goal, but the eruption of scandal that ensued eliminated any possible reward.

Why does intention setting yield drastically different results than goal setting? Unlike goals, which are focused on the future, intentions are focused only in the present moment, the right now—this is a big key to success; we can never really accurately predict the future, but we do know what the present moment looks like. Intentions are oriented around the present, and this is the genesis of its power. You do not have to wait for an intention to materialize. Intentions are the basis for effective change and self-hypnosis. Intentions represent that which is most important to you.

Many times, when people set, for example, a weight-loss goal, they resort to unhealthy methods to hit that goal—they take pills, they forgo meals, they exclude essential nutrients—because they mistakenly prioritize a number over the process. These people almost always regain the weight they lose.

By setting an intention instead of a goal, the results are far more obtainable and reframed positively, for example: "I choose nutrient dense foods in greater quantity and choose to increase my daily activity." Your mental focus is now on the solution, not the problem. You do not have to wait for success, you can step into success today by choosing to create it with your intentions; this simple act will immediately create a sense of satisfaction and increase your happiness, letting go of any pent-up frustration from a feeling of underachievement previously.

The result: By intention setting rather than goal setting, you are more likely to create lasting change.

As a licensed psychotherapist who has helped countless clients live their best life, I have found that goal setting often amplifies failure, pain, and feelings of inadequacy. As a business consultant, who has helped both large and small businesses unleash their greatest potential, I have found that the teams I work with who abandon goal setting and start setting intentions are performing more successfully.

The heart of self-hypnosis is setting intentions. Here is how you can do it.

The Self-Hypnosis Solution

How to Set Your Intentions

The starting point for any change is to see it as possible, to believe in it, and to have faith that it is now manifesting into your desire. This is an intention. Intentions setting is actually far easier than goal setting, and far more powerful.

A good intention begins with the phrase "I am"; you must own it. No one can say "I am" for you. Unlike goals, which are often imposed by someone else, intentions come from within you. This is why effective self-hypnosis must begin with intention.

In the introduction, I asked you to write down why you purchased this book. I asked what you hoped would come true. I hope you have already written something down. If not, go back and do so now. This book is a guide, and like any other map, it works better when you follow it. It is from those written words that you will derive your first intention.

Now, close your eyes for a moment and envision what you wrote as a reality. You can visualize the paper or screen you wrote on in your mind, or you may hear yourself saying the words in your head. It feels pretty good to do that, doesn't it? You have not even been taught your first method of self-hypnosis, yet you are already using the power of your mind to create a new reality!

In your statement perhaps you wrote something personal, like: "I want to learn new things and help other people." Perhaps you wrote something focused on behavior such as, "I want to stop procrastinating." Maybe you wrote something to help you in business, "I want to open my own small business and stop working for others." Whatever you wrote, it is your starting point for going through this book. It is your dream or your goal. But now let us activate it in the present moment and turn it into an intention.

If your goal was to learn new things and help other people, your intentions may look like this:

- I am open to new ideas
- I am creating new experiences
- I am helpful towards others

There is genuine power in these intentions.

Because I teach many hypnotherapy certifications classes in both my Las Vegas and Dallas learning centers, I often meet people who hope to learn how to hypnotize others and I help them develop this skill. Far too often, these students wind up taking several classes from various instructors, but never seem to start their own practice. They go to conferences and events year after year, but never share what they have learned with real clients through hypnotherapy.

What is holding them back from actually doing the work they seem to be so passionate about? Well, it is a mind trap that comes from goal setting. They believe they cannot help others until they hit their goal of learning everything! They are not comfortable or confident in their abilities until they take hundreds of hours of classes. But reality is far different. First, it is impossible to ever learn everything about hypnosis, it would take multiple lifetimes. I have been doing this for more than 30 years, yet I still learn new methods and insights all the time. Never ever stop learning.

Second, they have a misbelief based on their goal—that until they take every class they can, they really do not have anything of value to share with others. This is another fallacy. Hypnosis is so simple a child can do it. While it is true a hypnotherapist should have proper training, disciples can share their knowledge with others so that other people can benefit as well. Even if it is just progressive muscle relaxation and direct suggestion, the ability to perform and share these procedures is valuable.

My students who goal set are obstructed by their inability to reach their goals. But my students who set intentions almost always begin sharing with others and helping people, even after the first day of class! Do you see the difference here and how important intention setting really is?

If your goal is to stop smoking, your intentions might look like this:

- I am caring for my health
- I am managing my emotions
- I am breathing well

You can do these three things right now. You do not have to wait to accomplish them. A lot of programs combatting smoking addiction have participants pick a quit date in the near future, which, of course, proves ineffective in most cases. In fact, if a smoker abided by these intentions, they do not have to frame it in a 'quit smoking' mentality, they can fixate on picking up something new in place of smoking—the results will be the same. If you act on these three intentions, you will intuitively not smoke.

My hypnosis clients will often come to my office believing that sessions will focus on their smoking habits. But in reality, I never really ask or tell them to quit smoking. Instead I refocus their intentions to a different lifestyle. They start caring for their health, saving money, tasting food, breathing easier, and accepting emotions rather than smoking them.

Years ago, I had a friend tell me she would never date a smoker. At the time, I smoked. I asked her why. She said, "That's easy! People who smoke cigarettes love the cigarette more than the people they claim to love." When I finally quit smoking decades ago, one of my intentions was "I am loving." I have not smoked in a long time.

If your goal is business related and you say you want more sales or more business, your intentions might look like this:

- I am motivated
- I am creative and discovering new solutions
- I am willing to do the work

Unlike goals, you do not have to wait for these statements to be realized; you can have more sales and better business today, by acting with intention.

The Self-Hypnosis Solution

Now it is time for you to write your intentions in the space below, to catalyze a new, positive perspective on your life. Start thinking about intentions that you can experience right now. By writing your intentions down, you see the answers to making change in your own handwriting. There is something very powerful about putting it on paper: it takes it from your head and authenticates it through tangible action.

List some positive intentions related to your hopes, dreams, and the changes you wish to make:

1) I AM _____

2) I AM _____

3) I AM _____

4) I AM _____

5) I AM _____

Chapter Two:
The Power of Self-Hypnosis

You have an inner voice that has been guiding you for as long as you can remember. Without structure for all our internal chatter, we lose a clear sense of what is important. This is the origin of procrastination and missed opportunities. This is a guidebook designed to help you make sense out of your internal dialog, and to reprogram your self-talk so that it inspires new behavior, lasting change, and drives you to take action.

Hypnosis allows its user to control their life—to be the director rather than the responder. This is the heart of the hypnotic suggestion. You want to make a change. You have probably been trapped by less than resourceful states such as anxiety, procrastination, ill health, or limiting beliefs. The hypnotic suggestions you will be giving yourself are tools for ending the automatic responses that have held you back. You will be discarding old ideas like, "I will show them how much I can eat and get the most out of what I paid for this buffet!" and adapting new ideas: "I am losing weight by choosing the best tasting, healthiest foods in the correct portion, even if my friends choose to gorge themselves at the buffet!"

In many cases, we are unknowingly hypnotized by someone else's interpretation of who we are or what they feel is best for us. These could be well intentioned messages from our parents or other caregivers, teachers, coaches, religious leaders, and even the media. When people in positions of power share ideas with us, our instinct is to accept it as truth.

A few years back I was sitting in a Las Vegas diner eating lunch with a friend who is a world-renowned magician. He was discussing the psychological predictability of a new magic trick he was planning to perform on a national T.V. show. When I asked him if he knew he could make it work, he looked at me and said, "99% of all people will believe 99% of what you tell them!"

That comment has stuck with me ever since. Marketers give us slogans and symbols that create mental associations in our minds. The result: When we have a coke, we smile! When we feel independent, we go to Burger King to "Have it our way!" And of course, everyone knows that the way to mark any achievement is with a crown—making Rolex the most well-known watch brand on the planet Earth.

Self-hypnosis is at work in your life, even outside of this book and the field, and it has been since your earliest memories.

Because of its overarching influence, its best to refine your understanding of the technique.

In order to implement the ideas in this book, we need to have a clear understanding that self-hypnosis is not only possible, but something you are an expert in already. To really understand self-hypnosis, you must dispel the myths created by Hollywood and ignorant skeptics who have never actually taken the time to learn the craft; embrace the truth that self-hypnosis can help you in almost any aspect of your life.

There are five fundamental truths about self-hypnosis you should be aware of, and by knowing these facts, you will arm yourself with the ability to access one of the most powerful tools for personal development, behavioral change, health and wellness, and emotional intelligence.

1. Self-hypnosis is a science backed approach to problem solving

Not only do academic and scientific journals support the effectiveness of self-hypnosis, studies including brain imagery and other methods of measuring mental and emotional responses clearly indicate that self-hypnosis produces real change, and not just a temporary placebo effect.

David Spiegel, M.D., Chair of Stanford University's Department of Psychiatry, has noted in his research that when we use self-hypnosis our brains reduce activity in other areas, allowing us complete absorption or focus. In hypnosis, our brains also create a mind-body connection that improves physical responses. This explains why hypnosis is so helpful in reducing symptoms of illnesses and accelerating recovery.

His research uncovered a third mechanism, dissociation between dorsolateral prefrontal cortex and the default mode network, which includes the medial prefrontal and the posterior cingulate cortex. The result: "During hypnosis, this kind of disassociation between action and reflection allows the person to engage in activities either suggested by a clinician or self-suggested without devoting mental resources to being self-conscious about the activity." His research has been supported by many other experts and demonstrates the very real scientific basis for the lasting effects of self-hypnosis.

2. Self-hypnosis is not sleeping and can be done even with the eyes open

Hollywood's portrayal of hypnosis often leads us to associate hypnosis with sleep. Hypnotists in movies often spread this misconception by saying overused phrases like, "Your eyes are getting sleepy!" or, "You are now asleep." In reality, hypnosis often involves relaxation, but one is never asleep and you are not required to be relaxed in order to experience hypnosis; this is good news for those with anxiety who find relaxation difficult. Believe it or not, you do not even have to close your eyes to experience hypnosis. Rather, it is a state of absorbed thoughts and focused concentration. One can use self-hypnosis training to combat insomnia and to transition from a hypnotic state into deep sleep—but this is just one use of hypnosis.

3. Self-hypnosis is not difficult nor time consuming

The value of self-hypnosis is not in spending long periods of time practicing the techniques. Meditation, which can be a form of self-hypnosis, is often believed to be more powerful when practiced for long periods of time. However, shorter periods of meditation are highly effective as well. The purposes of self-hypnosis and mediation are not to elongate your time in that state, but rather to benefit from the practice by applying your discoveries to the real world!

You can look at it this way: The purpose of practicing meditation is to transform life into a mediation. The purpose of self-hypnosis is not the self-hypnosis itself, but to take from the experience so you can make your life hypnotic! The goal of this book is to help you apply certain techniques to your intentions and drastically improve the quality of your life. This is the end result of hypnosis, living hypnotically and applying your knowledge in the practice across a variety of situations and circumstances. In other words, the purpose of hypnosis is not hypnosis, it is to become hypnotic!

In my previous book, *The Seven Most Effective Methods of Self-Hypnosis*, I share techniques that range from short practices to longer meditations.[1] Any of those techniques will work. In the next few chapters, I will be introducing some new techniques—some lengthier, but all will be valuable.

---

[1] Richard Nongard, *The Seven Most Effective Methods of Self-Hypnosis* (2019).

4. Trance is a natural experience

People are often amazed by the results of self-hypnosis and believe that the trance states associated with hypnosis are hard to create. Hypnosis is often described as an "altered state of consciousness." The problem with this description is that we associate an altered state of consciousness with something unnatural or even otherworldly. Hollywood movies often depict hypnosis as a phenomenon that catapults people into incredible, previously unexperienced states of consciousness, but in reality, the definition of an altered state of consciousness is much more mundane.

In self-hypnosis, the altered state is simply moving from an unresourceful state (stressed, anxious, unproductive, self-doubt) to a resourceful state like taking action, focused attention, selective thinking, or even happiness and joy!

Any phenomena that happens in hypnosis can also happen in the world outside of hypnosis. The altered state is not a mystical otherworldly condition; hypnotists use trance to act with intention, remove limiting beliefs, and set in motion something more effective and powerful. Hypnosis taps into that which is inside of you, the strengths, and resources that you already possess, and uses them as the source of power for creating lasting change.

When you use this guidebook, you will experience powerful shifts, and learn to utilize trance, but you will still be you. There will be no out of body experiences (unless you tap into your imagination resources) and no negative side effects, because trance is a natural experience.

5. Self-hypnosis will make you a better person

So many people go through life just reacting to what happens and never really "making it happen." When you learn self-hypnosis, you become one who makes it happen. The results will be seen in your work, your parenting, your personal performance, and even in your relationships.

Over the years, many clients have come to me to address a specific area of need, but by learning self-hypnosis, they discovered the true benefits extended far beyond their initial reason and permeated into almost every area of life.

One client who came to see me many years ago was an attorney; he wanted to address his lack of confidence in public speaking. He applied what he learned through hypnosis into all aspects of his life and reaped the benefits: he lost weight, increased his daily activity, and started mentoring others through corporate wellness programs. He eventually took my professional hypnosis certification course and is now an ICBCH-certified professional hypnotist. Although he still works as an attorney, he has a small, part-time practice shares the techniques of self-hypnosis with others. His life has transformed. He will tell you self-hypnosis saved his marriage by helping him develop increased empathy and emotional resilience, helped him be a better parent, and even a more persuasive attorney.

The Self-Hypnosis Solution

The human mind revolves around self-preservation. This is a trait that comes to us from millions of years of evolutionary biology. Unfortunately, it deters many from ever trying self-hypnosis. Our mind wants to protect us, so this inner voice tells us, "You can't try that now," or, "If you do this, bad things could happen." The result of this mind-trap is that we do not take risks—we play it safe. This mindset is also explains why entrepreneurs never start their own business and instead opt for the security of a paycheck, why depressed people don't get out of bed in the morning, and why we give up on attempting to surpass our self-imposed limitations.

Self-hypnosis is so easy even children benefit from it! In a study done at a pediatric pulmonary center, children as young as six years of age were taught self-hypnosis. An amazing 95% of these young patients, who were treated for anxiety, cough, chest pain, dyspnea, or inspiratory difficulties, experienced improvement or overcame their symptoms (Anbar & Geisler, 2005).

In 2016, members of the US Olympic Swim Team were given self-hypnosis recordings created by my friend, Dr. Steve G. Jones, and myself. The team won 33 medals, 16 of which were gold, and ranked number one in the world! We received reports that swimmers who listened to these self-hypnosis training tools felt as if the self-hypnosis sessions made a big difference in their overall performance.

Self-hypnosis is not magic, but it is powerful. We use hypnosis in our daily life, whether we know it or not. Scientists say we have over 50,000 thoughts a day. Many of these thoughts are self-talk statements, and in a way, these are hypnotic suggestions. We tell ourselves what we can't do, what our limits are, and what we can achieve. We talk to ourselves constantly. Sometimes this self-talk is a literal internal voice, sometimes it is just a partial thought or an awareness. Ultimately, self-talks are what drive our actions.

Chapter Three:
The Easiest and Fastest Method of
Self-Hypnosis

The 3-2-1 Reset Technique

For over 30 years, I have been using this method of self-hypnosis to control anxiety. There was a point in my own life, many years ago, where I was paralyzed by anxiety, fear, and turbulence. I was afraid to fly on airplanes, I was afraid to drive in traffic, and I seemed to be afraid of my own shadow. As a result, I missed many opportunities in life.

I share some of my story in a TEDx talk in Oklahoma City in 2019. You can access a recording of my TEDx talk on my website, **SelfHypnosisSolution.com**. This website also provides additional resources you can supplement this book with; you can make printable copies you can write on, if you have the eBook or audio version.

Although I rarely suffer from unwanted anxiety at this point in my life, I continue to use this self-hypnosis technique to take time out from the busyness of life to manage stress and provide clarity in decision making. Over the years I have taught this technique to many clients. They tell me that because the technique is so simple and so fast, they have been able to benefit from it immediately. I have taught it to anxious clients, depressed clients, clients who are trying to discover their core values, executive who must make decisions, athletes who want to get "in the zone," people who have to speak before an audience, and students who have important upcoming exams. In fact, I teach this to most of my clients and there is always an immediate benefit.

It is called the 3-2-1 Reset Technique, because there are only three simple steps and it will leave you feeling refreshed with a new sense of optimism and stress-free energy.

You can be either seated or standing for this technique. To begin, find a quiet, comfortable setting. It is crucial that you turn off all distractions: your computer, tablet, T.V., phone, or smart watch—shut the door if need be. The reason this is important is that in self-hypnosis, even a quick process like this, we should dedicate ourselves to it completely. Distractions are like a tap on the shoulder—we can't not turn around to see who it is. So, it is always best to minimize these, even for a few moments. Here are the 3 quick and easy steps to follow when preparing for your 3-2-1 Reset session,

Step One: As you read these words, simply scan your body and release any obvious tension you are holding onto. Pay attention to your breath. While you do this, count the next three breaths. You can do this with your eyes open if you are reading. As mentioned previously, accessing the state of self-hypnosis is not dependent on the eyes being open or closed.

You do not have to breath in any special way; you can breathe quickly or slowly; you can breathe deeply if you want to; the most important thing is to just breath and to count the three breaths. This step is all about grounding yourself and being present in this moment.

Step Two: Take your two hands and cross them across your upper body, placing the left hand on the right upper arm, and the left hand on the right upper arm. This is almost a self-hug. If you've been to yoga practices, you're probably familiar with this pose. The self-hug is widely advocated because it connects our physical experience to the inner experience. Research actually shows that this self-hug position can trigger physiological responses and release the chemicals in the brain associated with pleasure, security, and well-being.

Some therapists, who practice methods of bilateral stimulation, also believe that by crossing the left side to the right side, we are integrating our thinking and our feeling mental capacities.

Step Three: Spend the next one minute (three breaths, two hands, one minute) in this position while you practice paying attention to the breath. Be an observer of the breath. Allow your breath to be your focal point. Each breath marks each moment. By practicing staying in the present, you are setting aside regrets of the past or fears of the future. During this minute, your mind will continue to think. After all, this is what minds do; like a fish swims in water, people swim in thoughts. Thinking is perfectly okay. So is being aware of emotions, and so is noting physical sensations. The practice that you are trying to cultivate during this minute is not stopping your thoughts, emotions, or sensations, but rather learning to not follow them and instead use them as a cue to return your attention to the present moment.

You can use a timer, or you can just guesstimate when a minute has passed by. It is also perfectly okay to spend more than a minute focusing on the power of this moment. When you are ready, let a smile come to your face and release your self-hug. You can congratulate yourself now. You have just done your first self-hypnosis exercise!

This is a very basic process, but one that is highly effective. By adding nothing to this process and simply using it to stop anxiety, practice mindfulness, and relax, it will be of value and serve you well for years to come. I have taught this to countless clients, and I have never had anyone exclaim, "OMG Richard! That was amazing! You changed my life! Thank you!" Rather, when I teach this to people, they typically have the same response you probably have. They say things like, "Okay, I can see how that is helpful." Or they say, "That was relaxing." Or simply, "Okay, I did it."

I wish that for most of my clients, the power of this technique was revealed in its introduction. What happens far more often is that when I tell my clients to practice this twice a day for the next two weeks, they come back with what I call "retrospective excitement." By practicing it, they realize the profound value in it.

Self-hypnosis is a practice. Like a musician who must practice his or her instrument before a debut concert, or a comedian who must memorize his scripts and practice his timing to make it appear spontaneous and natural, self-hypnosis requires practice. You will need to be committed to this practice to derive the results, but I promise you the results can be profound.

I provide a practice video of this technique on **SelfHypnosisSolution.com.** You can use it to guide you twice a day for the next couple of weeks.

To help you with your commitment to practice, write down the two times a day that you can commit to this one-minute exercise. Before breakfast? After walking the dog? Before bed? Before a meal? By committing to a specific time, you will be far more likely to be diligent in your practice.

Stop reading right now and bring up your online calendar. Enter into your daily schedule the times you have chosen, and then set your daily alarm.

Of course, you are not limited to practicing this twice a day. You can do it as often as you find benefit. Some of my clients with anxiety or fears use this method 10-20 times a day. The more you practice, the more it will benefit you.

Let's take this simple technique to the next level!

We can build on this basic strategy and use it to produce lasting change. Although simple, this process can become quite profound. You can actually integrate any method of self-hypnosis into this basic process, or use the many other techniques I cover in my previous book, *The Seven Most Effective Methods of Self-Hypnosis*.

The value in step one is a grounding technique. To step into intentions, we should be well grounded. During step one, as we breath, we can breathe in our intentions, and exhale anything known or unknown that is holding us back from taking action. Let's say your intention is: "I am resilient." In this case you could breathe in saying "I breathe in resilience" and you could exhale affirming that saying to yourself, "I am calm" or any useful affirmation.

Affirmations are powerful tools in self-hypnosis. They activate our core values and validate our intentions when we speak them out loud. Almost everything that exists was spoken into reality at some point. What were your intentions in Chapter One? These can be spoken during step one.

We can also expand step one to include belly breathing or diaphragmatic breathing. Belly breathing is a specific method of deep breathing, which is associated with health and well-being. In fact, just doing step one with these breathwork techniques can have significant, lasting impact. UCHealth (University of Colorado Hospital) says: "Deep breaths are more efficient: They allow your body to fully exchange incoming oxygen with outgoing carbon dioxide. They have also been shown to slow the heartbeat, lower or stabilize blood pressure and lower stress."

Before we go any further, I want you to take in a deep breath. Go ahead, breathe in deeply and then exhale. What happened? If you are like most people, you puffed out your chest, perhaps arched your back, and took in a gulp of air. It probably produced a tightening of the neck muscles, and maybe even tension into the head. I have done this with thousands of people, and for most, when I simply ask them to take in a deep breath, this is the result.

The problem with this is that it produces muscular tension and puffing up the chest actually reduces airflow to the deepest part of the lungs.

To take deep breaths correctly, sit in a chair with your back, neck, and head in alignment. Place one hand on your belly. Imagine a balloon without air is in your belly: breathe in as if you are filling the balloon with air and exhale as if you are letting air out of the balloon. Do you notice a difference?

The difference is that you did not tense any muscles, you remained relaxed. You drew the air into the deepest part of the lungs, and this, according to Jerath, Edry, Barnes, and Jerath (2006), creates "(a) the presence of decreased oxygen consumption, decreased heart rate and blood pressure, and (b) increased theta wave amplitude in EEG recordings, increased parasympathetic activity accompanied by the experience of alertness and invigorating."

If you are looking for a pathway into hypnosis, this type of breathing can be a hypnotic induction in and of itself.

Try the 3-2-1 Reset again now. This time, adding the belly breaths.

Did you notice a difference? What benefits do you notice when you try belly breaths? Identify any specific benefits you noticed from doing it this way.

This alteration exemplifies another facet of self-hypnosis: you can add or change any component of your technique at any time depending on what best suits you. Self-hypnosis can be simplified, or simple practices can be extended or revised to elicit profound experiences.

Taking step two to another level

By placing two hands on the opposite shoulders/upper arms, you are giving yourself a self-hug. This can be enhanced by opening the palms and giving yourself a soothing touch. This is similar to a hypnotic technique called Havening, and it is believed that this type of touch creates a brainwave pattern that can help us to heal from trauma and pain.

As an anxiety control technique, the open palms in a figure eight across the upper arms can generate instant calm, reduce panic, and assist with emotional control. The process of this "self-petting" can be a few seconds to a few minutes. Experiment with this added technique and notice how it helps you. In what ways does this added technique change your experience?

The self-hug is important. It provides a mind-body physical connection. People often assume hypnosis requires stillness. This is not true. Stage hypnotists have long demonstrated hypnosis with people actively engaged in skits, and in clinical hypnosis, creating a physical connection to thoughts can be transformative. This is certainly true in self-hypnosis as well.

Supercharging your one-minute hug with true mindfulness and transformation

When one truly masters mindfulness, which requires practice, the results are transformative. Mindfulness transforms us by training our mind to live in the present moment rather than regretting the past, ruminating about mistakes, and/or fearing the future. Our minds are constantly scanning our past experiences to predict the future. This is an evolutionary trait that has served us well to avoid plagues, being eaten by a wild animal, and preparing our food for the harsh seasons. But in the modern world, it can lead us to losing sight of the present moment, the most important moment.

Not only does the mind scan the past to assess our present circumstances, it jumps the gun and attempts to predict the future—this is the heart of many of our problems. After millions of years of human evolution, we have a subconscious mind that can, in any new situation, assess decades of previous experience and reason to make a predictive computation and give us a behavioral or emotional action strategy in literal seconds. It really is amazing! But unless there is a bear in the forest, or some other threat that requires instant action, it can be a mind trap. This process causes us to miss the present moment, where the real power resides. When you learn self-hypnosis, which revolves around mindfulness, you are learning how to act with intention.

In my book, ***Turn Around Trauma***: *How to Live Your best Life After Adversity*, I point out three mindfulness exercises that make it valuable to self-hypnosis:

- First, the practice of directing your attention to your breathing.
- Second, practicing how to return your attention to your breathing anytime you notice feelings, thoughts, or sensations. The goal is not to stop thinking, stop feeling, or to stop having sensations. The purpose is to simply

note when you do this and to practice bringing your attention back to a focal point, in this case, your breathing.

- The third part of this practice is to begin to notice how easy and natural it is to revert our attention to the present when we notice our thoughts drifting into either the past or the future. Notice, during this week, times when you mindfully and intuitively return to the present from distressing thoughts, feelings, or sensations.

Although the practice of mindfulness is significant on its own, many people choose to add a period of self-reflection or positive affirmations to their self-hypnosis. By adding self-reflection, you can determine if your actions are in alignment with what is most important and reevaluate your choices.

I coach many clients, both online and in my office, using a technique of values clarification. You can add this component to your 3-2-1 Reset.

A big part of self-hypnosis is creating a valued direction and developing a method of living in congruence with those values. When one is congruent with a valued direction, unwanted and distracting behavior is decreased. The following is a process for identifying those core values that you can add to the end of your mindfulness routine:

> *As you relax into this moment, imagine you have just received a present. Imagine the present is a surprise. You do not even know who sent it, but you are now holding it. It won't be a simple gift,*

but rather a magical gift. It is the one thing you want more than anything else in life. Maybe it's big or maybe it's small. It might even be too big to hold. It is your present, so you can see it any way you want to. You can even hear the present. When a child is trying to figure out what is inside of a gift, they often shake it. You can even do that in your mind, hearing the gift inside of the box. Feel the shape of the box. Is it a square, a rectangle, or an irregular shape? You can begin to open the gift. Inside the wrapping, you find exactly what you wanted more than anything else. Perhaps it's the deed to vast and beautiful lands, a diamond worth millions of dollars, or even the winning lottery ticket for 100 million dollars. This is your gift and you can imagine it however you'd like. Therefore, go large and take this opportunity to discover what you would want more than anything else, if you were to receive a magical gift. Allow yourself to dream big, opening the present and enjoying the magnificent gift inside. Now that the wrapping paper lays to the side, hold that gift in your hands, or place the gift out in front of you, and breathe. See your gift and imagine all of the changes in life that will come as a result of receiving this gift. How will you feel? What experience will it bring? Will it bring a sense of freedom? Will it bring the respect of others? Will you now be able to help others? Will the gift help you be more secure or even feel more important? Continue to explore this idea in your mind. Having this gift will allow some of your deepest needs to be met. What are they? Become aware of them. Note the words that come into your mind that describe these needs. Note the feelings you associate with this gift. Now open your eyes. What two or three words come to mind?

35

Close your eyes again and breathe, noting the feeling of that breath as you relax even further. It is interesting how what we truly value or need is often represented by something tangible. However, with a little reflection, we soon discover what is most important is not the gift itself, but what the gift represents. You described what you valued most as _____ and _____.
These core values are your valued directions.

Chapter Four:
Adding in the Power of
Affirmations

What we tell ourselves is really the heart of self-hypnosis. Self-hypnosis comes from the tradition of autosuggestion. Émile Coué, a pharmacist, pioneered a technique for programming our mind with affirmations. What he discovered about self-talk was amazing: he noted that when he gave a positive affirmation or suggestion about medication, patients found greater benefit to the medicine. It acted faster, had greater effect, and helped them more. It was from this experience that Coué identified the value of suggestion in hypnosis.

Suggestion is really an affirmation. Self-suggestion is the heart of self-hypnosis. What do you want your hypnosis to produce or result in? These wants and needs can be framed as affirmations, and by adding another minute for affirmations to your mindfulness routine, you can magnify the power of self-hypnosis. Later in this book, we will explore multiple methods and ways of creating affirmation.

One of my favorite quotes is from the bestselling book, *The Power of I Am and the Law of Attraction* by RJ Banks. In it, he writes, "If you'd like to know what your life is going to be like five years from now, simply look at what you're saying about yourself right now."

That's really important to note. I do not think that's simply a cute quote from a book, I think it's a real actionable strategy. Our affirmations should be centered on the present moment. In fact, I am going to give you five P's for successful affirmations:

1. Present: Affirmation are present tense, based on intention.
2. Personal: Affirmations are about you and begin with "I."
3. Powerful: Affirmations expand our thinking and challenge us.
4. Peaceful: Affirmations are congruent with a better world—not only for us, but for the people around us as well.
5. Proactive: Affirmations access resourceful states that encompass the previous four P's.

In accordance with the first P of successful affirmations, an affirmation needs to focus on the present. I am healthy. I am successful. I am abundant. Those are simple affirmations, but they are highly effective. Now, look at the problem of cognitive dissonance: What if I do not believe my affirmation? By simply speaking that affirmation out loud, you are literally creating that experience. Even if we didn't have money in our pocket, at the moment we state an affirmation such as, "I am wealthy," we've brought attention to the wealth that is inside of us and that wealth will always multiply if we are focusing on the present.

The second P states that an affirmation needs to be personal. It is about you and you only. I highly recommend short "I am" affirmations. We can trace back the use of the phrase "I am" to biblical history; God uses "I am" numerous times—he even claims it as his name to Moses at the burning bush (Exodus 3:13). No matter your religious preference, "I am" has persevered through history as a significant way to phrase things in order to create a new experience and a new reality.

As the third P underlines, affirmations are powerful. I think it's important we challenge ourselves; if you're uncomfortable with some preformatted affirmations in an affirmation book or tape, because you're not quite sure if you're entitled to those affirmations yet, I encourage you to challenge yourself. You can always write your own affirmations, short-term focused and of things you have full confidence are within your current capabilities. Challenge yourself. Use affirmations that push yourself, that cause you to step outside of your comfort zone and into a new, joyful experience.

The fourth P is Peaceful, because that is what affirmations are. We need to strive for peace. We need to strive for harmony. So, if you have conflict with another person, your affirmation should not be about them, it should be about you.

Example: "I am grateful for an opportunity to learn from different, or difficult, people."

When we inject gratitude into areas of conflict in our lives, not only do we find resolution, but we step into abundance in our interpersonal relationships as well.

The fifth P is crucial. Affirmations are proactive. In other words, I want to use affirmations that create resourceful states. "I am physically well. I am balanced. I am of clear thought. I am sober." Never underestimate the power of sobriety. I love it when people are getting high on life rather than mood-altering chemicals.

Now, of all of the different types of linguistic patterns for affirmations, I think many people fall into the trap of using affirmations that are future tense. They create their affirmations to predict what's going to happen in the future, though the reality is that the future is unpredictable.

Our impact lays in the "right now," being conscientious of what we say about ourselves, our experience, and our perceived reality will produce results—it's going to produce rewards and successes, if we choose.

I have heard an expression related to anger: "You have the same pants to get glad in that you have to get mad in!" It may be a trite little saying, but I think it speaks a truth. We have the ability at any time to create a new state, to step into abundance, to step into prosperity, and to use affirmations to proactively generate resourceful states.

Affirmations are powerful elements of self-hypnosis. They create reality when spoken. They create congruence between beliefs and behaviors and lead to lasting change. Affirmations are the heart of autosuggestion, which in turn, is the heart of self-hypnosis. They set into motion powerful mechanisms of both mind and word that lead to action. By adding affirmations at the conclusion of our mindfulness exercises, we are literally moving forward into a new reality.

Chapter Five:
A Strategy for Self-Hypnosis Induction

In this chapter, I am going to share with you a comprehensive and easy to follow process for self-hypnosis for those who have not yet discovered their favorite method, or for those who are looking for something more effective than what they are currently practicing.

As you learned in Chapter Three, the 3-2-1 Reset is a great technique that, like any other self-hypnosis technique, can be elaborated on to become as long or as short as desired, or as simple or intricate as desired. It can be applied in different ways, including as a self-hypnosis induction. However, any self-hypnotic method you know can be applied to the ideas in this book.

I call my skill-building induction my "go-to" process for self-hypnosis, because each component of that technique contains a lesson or a skill. Over the past 30 years, I have taught this skill-building hypnosis induction to thousands of people. The results have been phenomenal. Even If one never goes beyond this experience by adding self-suggestions, affirmations, or other processes of hypnotic suggestion, but only practices this hypnotic induction, the results are effective. This is because the induction itself teaches the skills of mindfulness, therapeutic relaxation, and taking control over both mind and body. In and of itself, this is a valuable practice. When I have had the luxury of adding to the induction processes in self-hypnosis, or training clients in moving beyond induction and into suggestive therapy, the results were amazing.

It is also important to note that you should not desire to create any specific outcome yet. What is most important is learning the process. You may feel as if this process is quite simple and that you access profoundly resourceful states easily, or, you may find that it is difficult and that you have trouble gaining access to deeper levels of the experience. Either outcome is acceptable. Often our expectations are colored by cinematic representations of hypnosis, or internet forums extolling profound out-of-body experiences or other manifestations of hypnotic phenomena. These are often unrealistic expectations.

Go into any process you are learning with an open mind by simply following the process and letting the outcome be as it may. As you continue to practice self-hypnosis, you will develop your own understanding of what hypnosis can do for you and what your full potential is.

The Contextual Skill-Building Induction uses basic components that can be combined with other methods. Certain components can be emphasized, and others shortened to tailor to the user's needs. Here are the basic components:

- Eye Fixation
- Progressive Muscle Relaxation
- Autogenic Training
- Mindful Awareness
- Breath Focus
- Visualization
- Direct Suggestion

The process begins by finding a peaceful environment where you can be free of distraction. Find a comfortable chair where you are well supported and comfortable. At any time during this process, you can adjust yourself for comfort, breathing, to swallow, to scratch an itch, or to meet any other needs that may arise. Those little distractions will not disturb you; they will simply help you to relax further in this time.

It is always best to set aside dedicated time for self-hypnosis. You will need to dedicate 10-15 minutes each time you practice this method when you are just starting out.

Eye Fixation

Once you have found a comfortable spot, look at the image on this page. It is a copy of *A Sunday on La Grande Jatte*, a painting by Georges Seurat. You may have seen this painting before—it is a famous example of pointillism, a style of art where the painter uses tiny little dots to make a larger image. Now, choose a place on this image to focus all your attention: it can be any of the dots, a dogs' tail, a woman's hat, the edge of the water, or part of a shadow. Stare at this one spot for at least 45 seconds.

Did you notice that by focusing on one single spot, your eyes got a little tired? This is normal; it is ocular fatigue. Hollywood hypnotists use a pocket watch as the point of focus, but it is the same principle. In fact, you can just use any spot on a far wall, no pocket watch or famous artwork required.

The Self-Hypnosis Solution

As you stared at the spot, did you notice the spot changed a bit? Perhaps it became hazy or fuzzy and seemed to disappear for a bit, or perhaps it became sharper and more focused while the background seemed to fade away. For some people, they notice no change, but what is really most important in this step as that you direct your focus to the present moment. In a way, this is practicing more mindfulness. The spot is here, right now, and the principle wisdom of this exercise is that *you have the ability to shift your focus at any time*, even to something as simple as a spot in a book, or a corner on a wall.

Think about this element of the practice. You have a challenge or concern that you have spent a great deal of time ruminating on and are attempting to resolve, but by fixating on a problem, you are stuck inside of it. By simply shifting your attention, even to something as simple as a dot, you have just learned how to easily move your focus. Learning to move away from distractions, problems, or physical or emotional stress is the key. Eye fixation trains us to focus our attention on the present. It is simple, yet profound.

For example: If you are having financial challenges and you want to utilize self-hypnosis to induce a financial or career breakthrough, you are on the right track. Up until now you have probably spent many hours focusing on how little money is in your bank account and how opportunity has not presented itself. By thinking about or focusing on the undesirable, you are actually aligning with poverty consciousness and what you are lacking, rather than attracting the desirable solution. Both your actions and your mind align with that which they choose to pay attention to, and many people self-sabotage their success and happiness by focusing on the wrong things in their lives.

Progressive Muscle Relaxation

The Contextual Skill-Building Induction continues with progressive muscle relaxation. In this part of the process, you learn the difference between tension and relaxation. This is important. Although relaxation itself has value, learning to intuitively notice the difference between tension and relaxation can change your life. Often, we subconsciously carry the day's tension in our bodies. The end result is that we do not know that we are in crisis because we are constantly carrying this tension and only super-stress diverts our attention to it. By learning to notice the difference, one becomes proactive and releases tension long before it becomes a health or emotional problem.

Right now, I would like you to prop the book up for a moment, or lay the book flat on the desk, table, or floor in front of you. Let both of your hands relax on the furniture, floor, or on your lap. Bring your attention to your hands and pay attention to the muscles in your forearms, palms, the back of your hands, and in your fingers.

Now, hold your hands in a tight fist.

Hold that tension for a few moments, you can even slowly count from 1 to 5. Now relax your hands slowly, letting your fingers open and rest in front of you. Do you notice the difference? Do it again. Curl your fingers into your palms and hold the tension as a fist for a few more moments—really let yourself feel it. Hold your fist tightly for another moment or two. Now, open your hands slowly, releasing the tension and letting your fingers relax again. Do you notice how relaxed your hands feel now? Did you notice that the second time you relaxed your hands, you doubled the sense of relaxation? The real value of this is in practicing awareness of the difference between tension and relaxation. Far too often our stress is chronic, and as a result, we grow accustomed to it and wrongly assume that our bodies are fine. This exercise will help you practice control over the physical aspect of tension.

Now scan the rest of your body: begin with the muscles in your eyes, your brow, and your face. Let them all relax. Unclench your jaw and let your face become relaxed. Let the relaxation extend down into your neck and shoulders. You may find it beneficial to rotate your shoulders and neck, and let all tension melt away. Continue scanning your body, detect any areas of tension, and let those muscles slowly relax.

After you relax the muscles in your face, neck, and shoulders, focus on each of these muscle groups:

Your upper arms and forearms

Your hands and fingers

Your back and spine

Your chest and belly

Your buttocks and thighs

Your calves and shins

Your ankles and feet

And finally, your toes

Ideally you should go through each muscle group slowly, really paying attention for any extra relaxation you can create. You will notice that your breathing becomes smooth and rhythmic, and your heartrate calm and regular. You will also notice a sense of physical well-being as you release tension.

You may also notice that your mind is occupied by thoughts. If this is your first time practicing this type of exercise, you may have many thoughts and emotions. You may feel anything from empowerment to self-doubt. Do not worry about this awareness even if you find it difficult. After all, we are supposed to think and feel, it is what the mind does. It would be unnatural not to have many thoughts. As I have mentioned before, a fish swims in water and people swim in thoughts. We will address those later.

Autogenic training

Autogenic training is similar to progressive muscle relaxation and, in fact, the two processes can be combined to enhance your experience. "Auto" literally means "self" and "genic" refers to generating or creating. So, the literal meaning of autogenic training is learning to self-create. There are formal training programs in autogenic training—it is often used in nursing and psychology—and many deeper levels that you can use as strategies for self-hypnosis by studying the discipline further. However, in this exercise, we are going to keep it simple and focus on creating two sensations that most find rewarding and simple to experience. The first being warmth, and the second being heaviness.

The best way to begin creating these sensations is to return your attention to your hands after doing progressive muscle relaxation. As you return your attention to your hands, pay close attention to them as they rest on your lap or the armrest of your chair. Now, think of the word "heavy." As you think of the word heavy, focus your attention on your hands and say, either out loud or mentally, "My hands are heavy." As you say this, notice an awareness of heaviness in your hands and repeat this process two more times: "My hands are heavy, my hands are heavy." Now, just allow your hands to be heavy.

Now think of the word "warmth" and as you pay attention to your heavy hands, say to yourself, "My hands are warm, my hands are warm," and let yourself notice warmth. As you focus on your warm and heavy hands, repeat your statement: "My hands are warm, my hands are warm."

As your hands continue to rest, say, "My hands are warm and heavy, my hands are warm and heavy." Notice any sensation of either warmth or heaviness in your hands. Again, say to yourself, "My hands are warm and heavy, my hands are warm and heavy."

It does not matter if you are only slightly aware of either warmth or heaviness or if it's an overpowering sensation. What is most important is that you have begun to allow yourself to create sensations and experiences, even at a minimal level.

The lesson here is profound. If you can create warmth or heaviness without anyone altering the room temperature or putting a weight on your hands, what else can you create? Do you think you could create joy and abundance? Do you think you could create wellness and health, or confidence in any situation? What you are learning here is that you have the amazing ability to create from within.

This is one of the guiding principles in self-hypnosis. Perhaps you came to hypnosis by way of failure and frustration. It might not feel like you have the resources within you to solve any problem. Fortunately, feelings are not of the same nature as facts. In self-hypnosis, you will discover that despite past difficulties or challenges, you have the amazing ability to create from within, and that your potential is unlimited. All of this is learned by starting with something simple—warmth or heaviness.

Mindful Awareness

As you continue to relax both mind and body, return your attention to your breathing. Notice any rhythm or pattern. You do not have to breathe in any special way, rather, be an observer of your breathing: breathe in and breathe out—don't try to speed up or slow down your breath, just simply pay attention to it

Each breath marks each moment. Any time you find your mind wandering and following a thought, a feeling, or a sensation, use this awareness as a cue to return your attention to your breathing.

The Self-Hypnosis Solution

As you practice focusing on your breathing, you will probably notice your mind racing with thoughts as minds often do. So many beginners in self-hypnosis seem disturbed by the fact that the mind is doing what it is supposed to do. It should be of no concern to you that the mind continues to think during moments of silence. Do not follow your thoughts during this practice, acknowledge them and use them as an indicator or a cue to return your attention back to your breathing.

Visualization

Using the creative faculties of the mind, imagine yourself in a wonderful place; perhaps somewhere you have been to before or hope to go someday, or even a mystical place of your own fabrication.

Now, imagine you are outside on a perfect day in this place, underneath a clear blue sky. As you gaze up into the sky, you notice a singular large, puffy, white cloud as it begins to float lazily across the horizon. Use your imagination to simply follow that puffy white cloud as it moves off into the horizon, becoming smaller and smaller. You will notice that as it shrinks with distance, it is easier to observe; you can easily shrug off any previous distractions, past regrets, or fears of the future, and simply focus on this moment. You can let go absolutely and allow that single white cloud to carry off any remaining stress or tension as it disappears into the horizon. Breathe in and breathe out.

That point when you realize that the cloud has completely disappeared out of sight is the point where we reach the resourceful state of hypnosis.

No matter which methods of self-hypnosis you find most beneficial to you, there is one aspect of learning self-hypnosis that is universal: You will need to practice frequently and regularly. Although some people have profound revelations in the first session or two, many do not. This reminds me of an old parable where the stream says to the river, "You go quickly, I go slowly but together we reach the sea."

Do not be disappointed if your expectations do not match your experience in the first few sessions, or even after months of practice. The fact is that self-hypnosis is a skill that needs to be honed, and each experience, no matter its depth, is a valuable opportunity to learn. Sometimes we do not see the knowledge until much later, but they will always materialize for someone who works towards them.

I am providing you with a free practice audio recording and a printable self-hypnosis script for the Contextual Skill-Building Induction which you access on my website, **SelfHypnosisSolution.com**

Chapter Six:
The 4-6-8 Breathwork Induction

The 4-6-8 method of deep breathing is a strategy that you can use to access the resources of the hypnotic state. In self-hypnosis, you can use any induction strategy of your preference; something like the Contextual Skill-Building Induction, explained in the previous chapter, requires five, ten, fifteen, twenty minutes each time to really build and access skills that combine mindfulness with progressive muscle relaxation, autogenic training, visualization, and creating from within the resourceful states.

Often though, people incorrectly think that self-hypnosis is a process which takes a great deal of time. In Chapter Three, I shared with you the 3-2-1 reset technique, which only takes as little as one minute to practice. I am now sharing the 4-6-8 method of deep breathing, which can be used as a very short hypnotic induction to take physical control of one's experiences at any time. There have been numerous studies that demonstrated the physical and emotional benefits of deep breathing. By engaging in deep breathing activities, we take control of the parasympathetic system within the body. We seize physical control of our experiences, which can be really useful to people who are dealing with anxiety, panic, a sense of chaos, or are feeling completely overwhelmed.

It's also a great exercise to start your day. Many years ago, I would begin the day by smoking a cigarette. A lot of smokers say that smoking calms them down—that is actually not true: Nicotine is a vasoconstrictor, a low-level stimulant. It actually excites us. It revs us up and gets us going. Then why are so many smokers misled into believing that cigarettes calm their nerves? The answer is simple—self-hypnosis. By smoking a cigarette, they are engaging in ritualized deep breathing techniques, albeit a very unhealthy one compared to yoga. With smokers who come into my office, one of my approaches is to teach them how to recreate the benefits of the deep breathing from smoking through a new set of strategies based on deep belly breathing.

I'd like you to simply take in a deep breath. Go ahead, breathe in deep, and then exhale. Use the same strategy we highlighted in Chapter Three: Do not just puff out your chest—imagine a balloon in your belly that you need to fill up once again. Do not tilt your head back, as this will restrict the air flow; keep your body in alignment with your chest relaxed. We have been breathing since the first day we were born and will continue to breathe till the last day of our lives, but deep belly breathing reimagines the actions we take for granted.

The Self-Hypnosis Solution

Once again, you are going to put your hand on your belly and breathe in deeply to expand your torso, and fill that balloon with air once more. Now, let the air out of the balloon. Repeat this process.

The 4-6-8 technique for self-hypnosis uses these belly breaths. We are going to breathe in for four seconds: We're going to count one, two, three, four. Then, we are going to exhale with a six count to let all of the air out: one, two, three, four, five, six. This allows oxygen to reach the deepest part of the lungs. It lets oxygen touch every cell in the body. It changes our physiology and brings us into a mindful place in the present moment, setting aside concerns of yesterday or fears of tomorrow.

We are going to repeat this eight times—four counts inhaling, six counts exhaling. Some may experience dizziness as they begin to practice therapeutic breathing; that is why it's important that you are in a stable place, sitting in a comfortable chair, perhaps with armrests.

It is okay if the first couple of times you do this, you only manage to repeat the four and six counts twice, four, or six times, but your ultimate goal is eight.

I replaced my former morning routine of smoking cigarettes with this technique. Now, I start my day by sitting on the settee at the end of my bed and practicing this exercise for three or four minutes. The breathing technique is, in and of itself, a valuable strategy; it is fine if that is all you do in the morning to start your day.

Just like we did with the 3-2-1 Reset method, we can enhance the 4-6-8 method with autosuggestion or the self-hypnosis suggestion techniques that I am going to be sharing with you in the later chapters of this book.

I would like you to practice this with me now. Let's go ahead and begin the 4-6-8 technique. Sit in a comfortable chair and close your eyes. You can take a starter breath to kick off the practice, and you can do this with your hand on or off your belly. Take in a breath, filling up that belly with air, counting one, two, three, four and then letting the air out. One, two, three, four, five, six.

Breathe in again, one, two, three, four. And out, one, two, three, four, five, six. Notice how good it feels to just breathe, to be present in this moment. It is perfectly okay if between each set of four and six you need to take a couple of shorter breaths. Now go ahead and breathe in again, filling that belly up with air. One, two, three, four and exhale, one, two, three, four, five, six.

When we take a longer time on the exhale than the inhale, we get rid of all of the carbon dioxide, all of the toxins, and anything else stored up in our lungs. We are opening our bodies for the next intake of four. One, two, three, four. Exhale. One, two, three, four, five, six. We have done this four times now, and if you're comfortable, continue on. One, two, three, four. Exhaling. One, two, three, four, five, six. One, two, three, four. One, two, three, four, five, six. Two more to go. One, two, three, four. Exhaling, one, two, three, four, five, six. And our last one, breathing in, one, two, three, four. Exhaling, one, two, three, four, five, six.

Let the eyes remain closed for a moment, breathing naturally. Just breathing in and breathing out, effortlessly breathing and focusing attention on it. Neither trying to speed up nor slow down the breath, not trying to breathe in any special way. Taking a moment to be fully present, practicing the art of mindfulness.

It feels pretty good to access the state of hypnosis through a physical exercise of deep breathing, doesn't it? It really is amazing how, by engaging in the 4-6-8 method of self-hypnosis induction, you can access the creative, intuitive, and committed parts of the mind. You can experience physical control and be conscious of your heart rate—calm and regular, smooth and rhythmic. Let a sense of well-being surround you.

Know that in each and every day, in each and every way, by dedicating yourself to the practice of self-hypnosis, you're getting better and better and better. Are you ready for the rest of our lessons?

Chapter Seven:
Your Next Level of Success

The heart of hypnosis has always been the ability to make lasting changes based on suggestion. Though relaxation can be a pathway to trance states, it is not the primary goal of hypnosis; the real value in hypnosis comes from accessing untapped inner resources to influence change in your life.

You may have heard the term "post-hypnotic suggestion" (PHS). These are actions that a hypnotist suggests during a session that the one who is being hypnotized will act upon when the session is over. Typical examples might be, "You will eat less and engage in more physical activity each and every day." A smoker might be given the suggestion, "Situations where you used to crave a cigarette will now trigger the forgetfulness part of the mind." When you encounter these situations, and you will, you will forget to smoke.

The Self-Hypnosis Solution

Although these are simple examples of PHS, they work, and people really do see changes in their behavior after hypnosis sessions. In fact, the results are often long lasting, even lifelong in some cases. It might sound amazingly simple—the hypnotist says a few words, and voila, he creates permanent change—but there is more at work here.

First, the suggestions are not suggestions from the hypnotist. Sure, he or she might be uttering the words, but all suggestions come from the client. When I am doing a hypnosis session, I spend each visit with a client, finding out what their challenges are, what their desired outcomes are, what has worked for them in the past, and what unique strengths they possess that could help them make a lasting change. It is by listening to these things that I can identify how my suggestions can be phrased to most effectively help my client. In this way, all hypnosis, even hypnosis in my office, is really self-hypnosis.

If you came to see me to decrease your anxiety while driving in traffic, your initiative to invest time and money into tackling this issue tells me a lot about your intention and your desire to make a change. By listening to you describe what triggers your anxiety and how you have dealt with it in other situations, I can give you suggestions based on what strengths you already possess and identify what strategy will be most compatible with your strengths. But these strategies, stated as post-hypnotic suggestions, are really already within you. I might teach you skills for controlling anxiety, like the 3-2-1 Reset technique; based on what you are doing today, I might structure suggestions so that, in some ways, they influence the future: I might say something like, "Just as you practiced in the office today, when you find traffic coming to a complete stop and your anxiety rises, you can take your hands off the wheel (as you are parked in non-moving traffic) and take one minute to practice the 3-2-1 Reset technique. And just as you benefitted from practicing it here with me today, you will benefit from practicing it in the future, in any situation that previously bothered you."

I could even continue and embed affirmations into the session. I could have you repeat the affirmations you identified in your intentions. Continuing this example, I could ask you to say, "I am calm, I am calm, I am calm."

As a hypnotist, I use many different strategies for hypnotic suggestion. In the office, I have the luxury of using metaphors, and teaching stories as indirect suggestion. For example, if you were frustrated by procrastination, I could share with you the parable I mentioned in Chapter Five, "The stream said to the river, you go quickly and I go slowly, but together we reach the sea." Your subconscious mind would resonate with its meaning, and you would internalize the ability to recognize that there is no need to procrastinate anymore, after all, the tasks have to be completed eventually.

Or I might share a well-known story, maybe one from Aesop's Fables. One of my favorite lessons from Aesop is the story of The North Wind and the Sun:

> *The North Wind and the Sun were quarreling about which was the stronger, when a traveler came along wrapped in a warm cloak.*

They agreed that the one who first succeeded in making the traveler take his cloak off should be considered stronger than the other.

Then the North Wind blew as hard as he could, but the more he blew the more closely did the traveler fold his cloak around him; and at last the North Wind gave up the attempt. Then the Sun shined out warmly, and immediately the traveler took off his cloak.

The traveler, exclaimed, "What a beautiful day!"

I might share this story during a hypnosis session on leadership, problem-solving, or with somebody experiencing difficulties in their relationship and learning that there are different perspectives.

You probably know this story; it is perhaps Aesop's most famous fable:

There once was a speedy hare who bragged about how fast he could run. Tired of hearing him boast, Slow and Steady, the tortoise, challenged him to a race. All the animals in the forest gathered to watch.

Hare ran down the road for a while and then paused to rest. He looked back at Slow and Steady and cried out, "How do you expect to win this race when you are walking along at your slow, slow pace?"

Hare stretched himself out alongside the road and fell asleep, thinking, "There is plenty of time to relax."

Slow and Steady walked and walked. He never, ever stopped until he came to the finish line.

The animals who were watching cheered so loudly for Tortoise, they woke up Hare.

Hare stretched and yawned and began to run again, but it was too late. Tortoise was over the line.

After that, Hare always reminded himself, "Don't brag about your lightning pace, for Slow and Steady won the race!"

Hearing this familiar story might teach clients to pace themselves while making change.

Indirect suggestions such as parables, stories, or metaphors might seem like an interesting approach to hypnosis, but the reality is, my clients tell me what stories, parables, and metaphors will work for them. In other words, even indirect suggestion originates with the client. In this way, all suggestion is self-suggestion. It is autohypnosis. Anything I can structure as a post-hypnotic suggestion in my office, you can structure for yourself at home!

When are suggestions used?

As you practice self-hypnosis, whether you use one of the longer inductions, like the Contextual Skill-Building Induction, or one of the shorter ones, like the 4-6-8 method or the 3-2-1 Reset, you can borrow strategies from mindfulness training. You will discover that mindfulness-based stress reduction is fundamentally a hypnotic technique, even though practitioners and guidebooks never use the word hypnosis. In fact, they would actually claim that the work that they're doing or the skills that they're teaching are not hypnosis. But as a hypnotist, I recognize that mindfulness is congruent, in many ways, to induction in the practice of hypnosis.

Most oncology centers in the United States offer mindfulness-based stress reduction training to cancer patients. Mindfulness-based stress reduction is utilized to assist in treating a variety of health complications. Once incorporated, many patients experience a notable decrease in the severity of their symptoms. They feel greater levels of emotional comfort during surgical procedures and they end up requiring less anesthesia. They can recover faster. These same benefits can be reproduced using self-hypnosis.

I think hypnosis is an umbrella term—it is multifaceted. There is stage hypnosis, authoritarian approaches to hypnosis, Ericksonian hypnosis, meditative hypnosis, etc. Mindfulness-based hypnosis is yet another facet underneath the umbrella.

Dr. Jon Kabat-Zinn, a researcher at the University of Massachusetts, wrote numerous books and given countless speeches over the last 30 years on mindfulness-based stress reduction. He has successfully instituted his method into a pain control treatment program that is now used in the medical field. He also identified seven elements of our attitude during our experience while practicing mindfulness. We can map these over to our practice of self-hypnosis:

The first one is to be nonjudgmental during the experience. You may hear yourself thinking, "What if I have to take a breath between my 4-6-8 exercises?"; or, "What if I can only take three breaths?"; or, "What if I didn't make it to eight repetitions and I have to lean back in my chair and just take a break for a moment?"; or, "What if I experienced an unexpected emotional release during a hypnotic process? Is that good or bad?" All of these thoughts are perfectly fine to have.

Things are just things, thoughts are just thoughts, and sensations are just sensations. It is great to cultivate a spirit of flexibility as you're practicing self-hypnosis and to be nonjudgmental about both the process and your ability to complete it.

As you learn and experience self-hypnosis, you will realize that there is no way to do anything perfectly. The best way to do it is to do it in the way that is most beneficial for you. If during a self-hypnosis session, you were expecting to be able to devote 20 or 30 minutes to it, but unexpectedly, you are called away after only twelve minutes, it doesn't mean the session was ruined. What it actually means is that you have the ability to benefit from the twelve minutes that you were able to dedicate to it. You must realize that tomorrow, when you have the opportunity to practice again, you'll be able to build on your acquired knowledge.

The second element is patience. We need to be patient both with ourselves and our expectations. The results, the promises of self-hypnosis, the mental health benefits, the emotional benefits, the physical benefits, and the metaphysical and spiritual benefits will always come to us—sometimes quickly, sometimes slowly. But they will always come if we dedicate time to cultivating the practice.

The third element is a beginner's mind: having curiosity or the desire for exploration. What is it like to pay attention to my breathing? What is it like to create a feeling of warmth or heaviness? What's it like to step aside from the busyness of every day and dedicate myself to a process of relaxation? What is it like to move out of a depression trance, an anxiety trance, or an anger trance and into a resourceful trance state where depression, anxiety, and anger are not present?

I meet clients who, after years of inaction, have actually become their depression or they have become their anxiety or become their anger. They are angry, they are anxious, they are depressed. And sometimes when they practice self-hypnosis and discover the freedom that it brings, it is an unfamiliar feeling to them. This is why a beginner's mind is important: You need to be comfortable with experiencing something new and exploring with a sense of curiosity for what you're seeing, sensing, and thinking.

The fourth element, of both mindfulness and hypnosis, is trust. Have faith in your own experience, not in a process. There are people out there who are seeking an elusive technique that will revolutionize everything for them. But it is not about the technique, it's about having trust in yourself in the deepest sense. It is about recognizing that you have the ability to do something impactful for yourself. Trust your intentions, allow yourself to be happy, joyous, and free.

Dr. Kabat-Zinn identified the fifth element as non-striving. Non-striving doesn't entail that we don't try or we don't seek out progress; non-striving means that we approach hypnosis and self-hypnosis at a natural, comfortable pace. It is a way of being. The goal of self-hypnosis is not to be hypnotized, and the goal of meditation is not to meditate: The goal of self-hypnosis is to become hypnotic, and the goal of meditation is become meditative.

Acceptance is the sixth element and the answer to all of our problems. Acceptance does not mean that we endorse, enjoy, or miss the negative aspects of the past, but it's a recognition of those things as they are. Realize that they brought you to where you are today. Despite the difficulties of the past, you move forward. The question for you is not where have you been, but rather, where are you going and what actions are you going to take to get there?

Our last element is non-attachment: not getting lost in the narrative. This is really important. Non-attachment is being able to put some space between you, your emotions, and your thoughts. If you think, "I'm not doing this right," "I'm not getting enough benefit from this," or, "The results aren't fast enough," put some space between you and those thoughts and the emotions they stem from. This is the concept of non-attachment.

These seven ideas can help free you as you learn, practice, and master self-hypnosis.

Chapter Eight:
The Art of Hypnotic Suggestions

I want to discuss how hypnotic suggestions work. Hypnotic suggestions are executed while the individual is under hypnosis. Post-hypnotic suggestions are intended to have their effects activate later on, after the individual comes out of hypnosis. In this chapter, you are going to start creating hypnotic suggestions to add to the inductions that you practice.

Let's say a client comes to see me to combat a smoking habit, just to make an easy example. They come in for a hypnotic session. I will guide them through a hypnotic induction, and then I'll give them hypnotic suggestions.

Let's say I've done the induction, and the puffy clouds disappear off into the horizon. Five, four, three, two, one. You have all heard a hypnotist count backwards. Five, four, three, two, one, zero. And then I make hypnotic suggestions. I might make suggestions in this case like, "And in the morning, rather than deriving your energy from nicotine, you'll derive your energy from oxygen. And before you do anything in the morning in the time that you used to have your first cigarette for the day, you'll sit on the settee in your bedroom and you'll practice the belly breaths that I taught you earlier. And you will discover that beginning tomorrow morning, it feels better to start the day with oxygen than it does nicotine." That is an example of a hypnotic suggestion.

Let me give another example of a hypnotic suggestion that I might give to smokers. Let's say they associate smoking with bowling alleys—maybe they're on a bowling league. I might say to them, "And you've done so well by becoming a nonsmoker today, and next Thursday when you're at your bowling league and your friends are smoking cigarettes, it will no longer be a cue to you to smoke a cigarette. In fact, it'll be as if you've never even smoked a cigarette in the first place. When they choose to make a choice that's different than the choice that you choose to make, it will no longer be a cue to you that it's time to smoke a cigarette while you're bowling. Instead, it'll simply be the choice that they've chosen to make, which is different than the choice that you've chosen to make, to breathe fresh air and to feel your very best. In fact, when somebody else lights a cigarette, I do not know why, but it might even be an indicator to you to forget that you ever even smoked in the first place. Act as if the idea is something completely foreign to you."

Another popular hypnotic desire is weight loss. A lot of people see me for bariatric hypnosis. I specialize in working with men who need to lose half their body weight. So largely, the folks who I work with are men, typically in their thirties or forties, sometimes fifties, who desire to lose half their body weight. My weight loss clients are 350, 400, 450, and even 500 pounds. I actually worked many years ago with the fattest man in America, and he was down to 711 pounds when I began working with him.

The typical scenario is that they have already tried multiple diets with no success. Perhaps they've had bariatric surgery and gained the weight back, or they can't qualify as a candidate for bariatric surgery because of other health complications. if they do not lose half their body weight, it's curtains for them. It's a death sentence. So, they are very desperate. They want hope.

And when they come in for that very first session, I give them hypnotic suggestions. I might suggest that they begin increasing their daily activity each and every day: "Take more steps today than yesterday, and more steps tomorrow than today." I suggest that they increase their daily activity until they reach 10,000 steps per day, which is a challenge for many of them. Typically, they start at around 2,000 or 3,000 steps a day, then begin working up.

I live in Las Vegas, the capital of buffets. There are probably more buffets per capita here in Las Vegas than anywhere else on the planet Earth. Most people see a buffet as an opportunity to prove they can eat more than $9.95 worth of food. So, I give a hypnotic suggestion, mentioned in Chapter Two, to my weight loss clients in Las Vegas because I know they're going to be going to a buffet eventually: "And when you go into the buffet and you grab your plate, you have an opportunity now to make any healthy food choices in the correct portion that will be best for you. And the good news here is even if other people choose to make a different choice, you will now be able to choose a meal that's most beneficial to you. You will no longer see the buffet as an opportunity to prove they underpriced it at $9.95, but as an opportunity to recognize it for only $9.95. You're able to get a healthy meal and the correct portion, even if the others who you are with choose to do something different."

Remember, these are examples of primarily direct suggestions. In my work with clients, I might use methods of indirect suggestions that I mention in Chapter Seven: stories, parables, metaphors, or poems. They can come from my personal experiences, or they can come from history. They can come from anywhere. They are intended to plant an idea in the listener's mind through meaning.

Let's say I have a client, an executive, for example, and he or she is trying to make some business decisions. In our economic climate, seizing control and making calculated decisions is a requirement of success. In my hypnosis session with that person, I might use one of my favorite techniques: retelling one of Aesop's fables, such as "The Tortoise and the Hare" and "The North Wind and the Sun," which were described in Chapter Seven.

A principle of the subconscious mind is that when we share a story, the listener will attach a meaning to it that is most significant to them. So, in hypnosis, I might use indirect suggestion as a strategy to have my client resonate with a subliminal message.

Now when people are learning self-hypnosis, they often ask, "But how can I do that myself? How do I give myself suggestions, direct or indirect?" You only have to look to the next chapter to find answers.

Chapter Nine:
The E.A.C.H. Sheet

I have prepared a worksheet for you, something that I call the "EACH Sheet." You write on an EACH Sheet for each hypnotic suggestion that you create. You do not have to hire a hypnotist to give you hypnotic suggestions; every hypnotic suggestion that a professional hypnotist gives you is actually something they coaxed out from inside of you, anyway. I do not make up suggestions—I listen to my clients. I hear what my clients have to say, and I make suggestions based on the resources and the strengths that they have, combined with what has worked for them in the past, what they've told me they'd like to learn, and what their desired outcomes are. It's easy to give yourself a hypnotic suggestion in self-hypnosis. You do not have to be dependent on any professional; you can create your own hypnotic suggestions.

E.A.C.H. SHEET

Dr. Richard Nongard

1.) Emotions you want to generate by aligning with your values

2.) Action you will take to create the outcome

3.) Change produces results—but you must look for change!

4.) How will you accomplish this (steps along the way)

Emotions

Because I value _____ I am
creating this emotional benefit _____.

Actions

With every opportunity I am _____
and I am _____.

Change

I am discovering (emotions) _____
with every _____.

How (Who, what, when, how)

When I am with, I will _____.

When I _____ I will _____

I will do this _____.

The Self-Hypnosis Solution

I recommend you print out four, five, or even ten copies of the EACH Sheet, as this is a proven and very effective way for you to structure your own hypnotic suggestions (free printable versions can be found on my website at SelfHypnosisSolution.com).

The way this works is simple: I utilize the hypnotic inductions that we have already covered in this book.

I love the Contextual Skill-Building Induction, even though it takes five, ten, or even fifteen minutes to complete. It teaches you valuable skills and it is an exercise I think you should be practicing each and every day.

You can choose to use a longer, classic module, such as the Contextual Skill-Building Induction, or a briefer induction. We can simply use a deepening technique to add on to each process. With self-hypnosis, the easiest deepening technique is to count from five to zero.

Now a lot of times people think, "What does number counting have to do with hypnosis?"—it has everything to do with hypnosis. It is a universal belief that when a hypnotist counts backwards, their volunteer enters a state of hypnosis; we see this in American movies like *Office Space* or *Dracula*. Bela Lugosi, who played Count Dracula, exemplarily said, "Look deep into my eye. Five, four, three, two, one." As part of a research project, I spent an entire day looking at movies produced in India, China, France, and various other countries around the world. No matter what country or culture the movie was from, whenever they portray a hypnotist, the hypnotist would count backwards. So, it's a universal association. Counting and counting backwards actually does facilitate access to the state of hypnosis.

When we finish a technique, whether it's the 4-6-8 method, the 3-2-1 Reset, or the Contextual Skill-Building Induction, we can maximize its resourcefulness by counting backwards.

Five. Each breath and each number marks each moment. Four. Three. And as you count down, avoid the temptation to count quickly; pace each number with each natural, slow breath. Two. One. Zero.

And now, acknowledge that it's at this moment that you've begun dedicating time for the improvement of your life: whether it's for your health, wealth, happiness, or any other area of life that's important to you.

It is okay to use your EACH Sheet during your hypnosis session. You can open your eyes and review what you have written. Your EACH Sheet gives you a set of self-hypnosis suggestions that you can utilize after your countdown from five. If you need to, and you can't remember them, simply open your eyes and read the sheet. The session will be perfectly fine regardless of whether or not you've committed your suggestions to memory.

Let's talk a little bit about what's on the EACH Sheet. EACH is an acronym to help you create self-hypnosis suggestions. And the first letter, E, stands for emotions that you want to generate to align with your values.

The Self-Hypnosis Solution

Let me give you an example: Compassion is one of my core values. Because I'm compassionate, I would like to feel a sense of joy. Because I care for other people, I would like to create shared joy. By affirming this in writing, I create security for my emotional outcome.

The idea is to concentrate on the emotions we would like to create or experience. Earlier in this book, you described and identified some of your intentions. This will lay the groundwork in self-hypnosis for identifying the emotions that align with your core values.

The A stands for the actions to create that outcome. It is really not the actions you're going to take, because that's based on the future. It is the actions you're taking right now, the intentions that we're stepping into.

The C in the acronym stands for the change that produces results. I meet people all the time who come to see me to treat depression or anxiety. They say, "But I'm still depressed. I'm still anxious." They have lost sight of the fact that they were more anxious and more depressed when they first came to see me. That change, whether it comes rapidly or gradually, is still change. Progress should be more important than feebly hoping for perfection. Change produces results, but we must look for those results. And the most amazing thing is when we look inside of ourselves for change, we will discover change. I believe that change will always result from emotions and actions that align with our core values

Finally, the H is how we go about accomplishing this. It is about the steps that we are going to take and the ones we are currently taking.

Your EACH Sheet is a fill in the blank, and this is for you to brainstorm.

In the Emotions: "Because I value _____, I'm creating this emotional benefit, I am discovering what emotions are important to me with every action." That's the fill in the blank, and the who, what, when, why, how. This is what helps you not to repeat the same behaviors in new situations that you exhibited in previous situations. This is relapse prevention. "When I am with _____, I will _____. When I _____, I will _____. I will do this."

Now, one of the things I want you to avoid in filling out the worksheet is using negative suggestions. "I will not overeat at the buffet" sounds like a great affirmation, but it is actually what is called a negative suggestion. With a negative suggestion, you are affirming what you don't desire. You should be looking for the positive suggestions, what it is that you desire: "I will eat a moderate amount of healthy choices at the buffet."

Let's fill out worksheet with an example. Somebody might come and see a hypnotist for pain control. Let's say that they have been experiencing chronic pain and they're learning self-hypnosis to help them manage their pain. "Because I value wellness. I am creating this emotional benefit."

"Security, satisfaction, joy. A lot of people have chronic pain and an absence of joy. So, because I value wellness, I am now choosing to create joy within me." This is a great hypnotic suggestion. You always want to keep it positive.

"Whenever I notice my chronic pain, it actually is not a challenge. It is not an obstacle. It is actually an opportunity for me to experience something different. So, with every opportunity, I am taking physical control over my body and breathing in, practicing mindfulness. And I am fully present. Change. I am discovering joy with every awareness of comfort in my body. The chronic pain client is always focusing on pain, never focusing on their comfort. When I am with my significant other, I will create joy. When I sit for a prolonged period of time, I will allow myself to notice comfort in my body. I will do this each and every time I'm presented with a new opportunity to create a sense of comfort where in the past it might've been pain."

Do you see how I filled in this worksheet using the example of chronic pain? The worksheet I have given you is sort of like the old Mad Libs game. Remember the Mad Libs game? You had a story and you filled in nouns, adjectives, superlatives, or whatever else, and then it would make a funny story. It really is the same thing here. And this is a way of creating hypnotic suggestions. What I would encourage you to do now is to take one subject, one area of your life where you would like to apply the principles of self-hypnosis and find lasting results and change.

We want to focus on just one subject, rather than every change we desire, because it is easier to pace ourselves this way. It could be chronic pain, creating wealth, creating joy, stopping smoking, getting better sleep, improving academic performance or sports performance—the list is endless. Whatever issue it is for you, I would like you to begin by really focusing on each method of creating your own self suggestions.

Before you begin your session, set your EACH Sheet out in front of you. Now, begin your hypnotic induction, whichever method you prefer, long or short.

At the end of your induction, add your ratification process, your deepening: Five, four, three, two, one. It is okay if you need to open your eyes to review the contents of your EACH Sheet, or keep them open the entire time. Read those suggestions to yourself.

Close your eyes again for a moment. You can even do what is called a transitional deepener, and you can ratify the state of hypnosis by counting again. Five, four, three, two, one, zero. You can open your eyes. The principle of compounding is that we give ourselves the same suggestions multiple times. Go through your EACH Sheet again. Go through each letter of E-A-C-H. Emotions, Actions, Change, and How. One more time.

Close your eyes and count backwards again. Three, two, one, zero. Look at that EACH Sheet and go through the suggestions that you would like to share with yourself. You should do this three times. Take as long as you need to internalize the suggestions you've given yourself, to feel your very best, and to allow yourself to be present in this moment. Stretch out any muscles that need to be stretched. And, when you are ready, open your eyes.

The preceding induction was an example of a short process, like the 3-2-1 Reset or the 4-6-8 breathing induction. This method might take five to ten minutes. Or, maybe you have chosen to use a longer induction, like the Contextual Skill-Building Induction. Those normally take ten to twelve minutes, eighteen to twenty minutes if you add these suggestions.

Practice this each and every day until it becomes second nature. When it does, I promise you will discover the same benefits of self-hypnosis that millions of people around the world experience every day, and you will begin living your best life.

Chapter Ten:
Three Things to do When You Hypnotize Yourself

Leaves on the Stream, Middle of Nowhere, and the Wayward Clock

In this book I have already stressed the importance of mindfulness in our 3-2-1 Reset method. Within this exercise, there is a minute of mindfulness where you just focus on your breathing. It's a great hypnosis induction that also teaches you the skill of mindfulness. At the conclusion of that one minute, we can extend the experience by using a number of different processes. We can extend any technique: If you are using the Contextual Skill-Building Induction, for example, you can use any of the three strategies I highlight below when the white cloud disappears in the horizon.

One of my favorite hypnosis books is *Get Out of Your Mind and Into Your Life* by Steven Hayes, the architect of ACT Therapy—

The Self-Hypnosis Solution

Acceptance and Commitment Therapy. One of the most fascinating things about this book is that nowhere within its pages is the word hypnosis or self-hypnosis used. But, the idea behind acceptance and commitment therapy is that we can create an experience of mindfulness and use it to put some space between us and our thoughts, sensations, or feelings. For example, if you came to self-hypnosis because you want to treat chronic pain, you can put some space between you and the sensation of chronic pain by mentally detaching yourself from the pain that you hold. I know many clients who become immersed in the emotions they experience; they become the depression that they feel, the anger that they have, and the anxiety that they hold. By putting some space between you and your depression, your anxiety, your anger or whatever the undesirable feeling is, you can just let those emotions be emotions without having to act on them.

Leaves on the Stream

Our first strategy is called ***Leaves on the Stream***, and it has always been one of my favorite mindfulness training exercises, and really, one of my favorite self-hypnosis exercises.

We begin our self-hypnosis session by setting aside the distractions of the world around you. Close the windows on your computer, turn off your cell phone, TV, and anything else that may distract you. Next, find yourself a comfortable place, relax, clear your mind and begin your Contextual Skill-Building Induction or the 3-2-1 Reset. Once you have reached your trance state, you will begin the Leaves on the Stream exercise to put some space between you and your emotions, physical feelings, or thoughts.

Go ahead and close your eyes, then take a breath and pay really attention to that breath to make yourself fully present in this experience. Pay attention to the chair below you, to your feet on the floor, to the air in the room around you. You can either sit in your chair with your neck and your shoulders aligned and your spine straightened so you can breathe into the deepest part of the lungs, or you might find it more relaxing to sink back into the chair.

You are now beginning to experience self-hypnosis in the way that's truly most beneficial to you. You've taken this time to acquire and benefit from the skills that you are learning, and so in the chair that you're sitting in right now, in this place, scan your body for any tension you might be carrying, and let that tension disappear.

Set aside any regrets from yesterday or any fears of tomorrow and mindfully pay attention to your breathing, letting your eyes gently close if they are not closed yet. Notice the sound of your breath, the pace of your breathing, and what it feels like to breathe air into the deepest part of the lung and to exhale. This is your time to learn, your time to experience, your time to use the creative part of the mind to help you master a new skill.

Use that creative part to imagine yourself next to the bank of a gently flowing stream. Observe the water, notice the earth around you, the sound of the stream, and how the current looks as it flows. Imagine some trees on the sides of the streams, both near you and far from you—different trees, different shapes, different sizes, different colors. Imagine that some of the leaves from those trees fall and land on the water, then watch those leaves float on the stream. This is all you need to do right now, just observe the leaves falling to the stream and floating gently on the water.

The Self-Hypnosis Solution

Spend a moment now to pay attention to your thoughts: What is it that you are thinking? Pay attention to your physical sensation: What is it you feel in your body? Pay attention to your emotions: What emotions are you feeling in this moment? Imagine placing any feeling, thought, or sensation that arises on one of the leaves as it floats across the surface of the stream. If you have an anxiety, you can imagine putting that anxiety on a leaf and letting it float. If you have a chronic pain or a hunger or a discomfort, you can let that float on a leaf. If it's a thought—"I missed out because I wasn't in the Zoom Room"—you can put that thought on a leaf. You can watch those leaves begin to float down the stream. It doesn't matter what you're thinking or what you're feeling or what you're sensing, or whether it is positive or negative, simply let all of them float.

If your thoughts stop at any time, just observe the stream; sooner or later you're going to think your thoughts again, you're going to feel your feelings again, you're going to sense your sensations again. You can let the stream flow at its own pace. Notice if you have an urge or a temptation to speed up or slow down the water in the stream. Let it flow the way that it will. Be sure to include any thoughts, feelings, or sensations that you have about this exercise that we're doing right now. Maybe the thought is, "This is wonderful and relaxing," or maybe, the thought is, "I'm not sure when I'll derive the benefit." Either way, let those sit on leaves and float down the stream.

If any of the leaves are stuck or do not move, rather than worrying and grabbing a stick to try to push those leaves along, just let them hang around. All you are doing is observing the experience that you're creating, and as an observer of the Leaves on a Stream, there's no need to take any action. If you find yourself following one of the thoughts, one of the feelings, or one of the sensations and forgetting about the other leaves on the stream, it is fine as long as you return to acknowledging each leaf.

You do not have to judge whether each is good or bad, just allow yourself to acknowledge it and watch it float. You can say to yourself, "Here's a feeling of anticipation," "Here's a feeling of restlessness," or, "Here's a feeling of focused concentration," and place those words on a leaf and let them float. It is normal during this process to lose track in this exercise, that is called Time Distortion in Hypnosis, and it'll probably keep happening. You might not know if a minute or three or ten have gone by, it really does not make a difference. If you notice yourself losing track of what you are trying to do, just bring yourself back to where you imagine yourself sitting and observing the leaves on the stream. Let those feelings, thoughts, and sensations gently float down the stream. Continue this vision for a minute or so, or however long you feel necessary to complete the process.

And with your next breath, pay attention to the feeling of the chair below you, your presence in the room, and to my voice. Let the image of the stream simply begin to dissolve as you open your eyes.

This has long been one of my favorite exercises with clients. It allows creativity, it allows creation, and it allows you the ability to put some space between you, your feelings, and your emotions. It follows a principle of mindfulness, non-judgment of intuition or creativity. I will provide a printed PDF of this script for you to use as a guide to extend the 3-2-1 Reset or the Contextual Skill-Building Induction into the *Leaves on the Stream* exercise.

The second and third procedures actually come from my book, *Richard Nongard's Big Book of Hypnosis Scripts*. A PDF is provided on the website. Again, you can place these pages in front of you as you practice; during self-hypnosis, there is no problem with opening your eyes and referencing a guide.

Middle of Nowhere:

Our next exercise is called the *Middle of Nowhere* technique. Sometimes, when we have a sense of chaos or feel overwhelmed, being able to escape is important to us.

After completing the 3-2-1 Reset, the 4-6-8 breathing technique, or the Contextual Skill-Building Induction, you can use this technique. By now, you are very familiar with how to access the resources of a state of self-hypnosis, so let's begin.

After you have removed any distractions, laid out your script papers, and settled in, close your eyes and direct your attention to your breathing. Let yourself relax and bring yourself to a state of self-hypnosis that we now know is so beneficial to you. A state of calmness, a state of serenity, a state of relaxation. If you find yourself distracted by anything around you—a noise from outside of the room, or a frustration from the day—you can return to this experience by simply redirecting your focus back to your breath.

As you breathe in and breathe out, neither try to slow down or speed up your breathing. Just breathe. By focusing on your breath, you are easily focusing your attention inward and letting go of any stress and tension that you might feel. Allow yourself to enter the resourceful state of learning, the resourceful state of creativity, the resourceful state of experience, self-hypnosis. Now, count backwards from five and with each number, simply become more present. Five, four... more creative, three, two... more relaxed, one, zero. Next, guide yourself through the following so you can transport yourself using imagination. The Middle of Nowhere technique is a great way to create a mental escape from all of the stress in the world around us. As you relax, you can recognize that a part of you is still in the physical world; you can feel the chair below you, your feet resting on the floor, and the gentle air.

At the same time, there is a part of you that needs to escape. It can drift away to a place of your own creation, or maybe even somewhere you have been before. A place that really is the middle of nowhere. A place that has no time, does not exist in the present, a place of your own creation, a place of your own experience in the middle of nowhere. But you have awareness in this place: Your inner voice, your guide of wisdom, your higher self is present. However, there is no awareness of pain, physical or emotional, in the middle of nowhere. It is simply an awareness of nothingness and in the middle of nowhere, nothing is just fine.

There is nothing to be, there's no expectation to be had, there's nothing to feel or sense. It's really quite pleasant to take this mental break for a moment isn't it? It's really quite pleasant to let a part of you drift above and from all the stress in your present situation, to a place of deep relaxation.

The lesson here is that at any time, in any place, we can use self-hypnosis as a way to rise up above and travel away from the things that have held you back from living your very best life. Pause your daily affairs in the real world for a few minutes to recharge. Then return to the present, this experience, the chair below you, and the air in the room around you. You'll discover that your creativity is a tool you can use to help you step into new experiences, new places, and a new sense of wellbeing. If your eyes are not open yet, you can go ahead and open your eyes, but if you need to stretch a bit or take a deep breath before you do, that's okay as well. When you're ready allow yourself to be fully present in this moment in space and time, open your eyes, smile, and observe the benefits of the exercise that you just did.

The Self-Hypnosis Solution

When it comes to hypnosis and self-hypnosis, everyone finds a different value and/or experience. What I'm sharing with you now are some ideas that you can use to possibly bolster your benefit.

Wayward Clock

The third process is called the *Wayward clock*. This is a way to detach yourself from the stress and the constraints of time that we have imposed on ourselves in a society abides by the clock.

Go ahead and close your eyes. Bring yourself to a state of hypnosis and relax into this moment, doubling the sensation of relaxation with each breath. Your heart rate is smooth, rhythmic, calm and regular. Now, unclench your jaw and relax your shoulders, let your hands become warm and heavy, and just be very relaxed. Pay attention to your next breath and let the air fill your lungs. Let your lungs be filled with oxygen and let that oxygen travel to every cell of your body to produce a sense of wellness in mind, body, and spirit.

Now in your mind, picture a clock—an analog clock, not a digital one. Now imagine that the hands of that clock read twelve o'clock. Imagine seeing that clock and realizing that it is no longer important what the numbers say. In fact, the hands of the clock could point to six o'clock or three o'clock or twelve o'clock, or the actual time when you began this exercise, it doesn't make any difference to you. And as you continue to relax, the meaning of time becomes less and less important to you. In fact, you can use the creative faculties of your mind so that instead of the clock going clockwise, you telepathically move the numbers on the clock; the nine can become a three, the three can become a twelve, and the twelve can become a six. You can imagine the clock being able to move from night today and day to night. You are no longer concerned about the time on the clock, but paying attention to this moment, the only moment that we have. After all, no matter what the hands on the clock say, the only time we actually have is right now. Pay attention to your breathing, pay attention to this moment, set aside any regrets of a prior time or fears of a future time, and pay attention to the feeling of wellness that you've created right this very moment by letting go of the numbers on a clock and accessing the resources that a state of hypnosis provides.

Let go of the constraints of time and place. This brings a sense of relief to every aspect of your life. Feels pretty good, doesn't it?

By learning and using these three methods, you can derive more enriched benefit from self-hypnosis.

Chapter Eleven:
Four Minutes of Forgiveness

Let me share an anecdote to start off our discussion on forgiveness. When I was six years old, I was afraid of the garbage truck. Early one spring morning, I was riding my bicycle over to my grandmother's house, which was not too far from where I lived. While on my big adventure to grandma's, I came face to face with a monstrous looking garbage truck that was emptying trash down the street. The loud noises, the clanging, the machinery on the truck—it was frightening. I was only six years old, and even the sanitation workers inside of the garbage truck seemed scary to me! They did not look like the people who I normally spent my time with, or that I knew personally. The workers wore beat up uniforms, they were strong, and they frightened me because they were different.

So when I passed the garbage truck, I sped up and began to peddle as quickly as I could. I was distracted by my overwhelming fear, so I forgot about the drainage grate in the curb just before grandma's driveway. Back then, the bars were vertical and consequently, as I drove over the grate, my front tire immediately fell between the safety bars and down into the drain. This resulted in the back tire jutting up and flipping over, throwing me over the handlebars. I landed on my chin, and unsurprisingly, I was all bloody and began to cry. One sanitation worker stopped the truck and ran over to where I was. He picked me up, gave me a hug, and held me. He carried me up to my grandmother's house and rang the doorbell.

My grandmother must have been freaked out, of course, at the sight of a strange man holding her bloody grandson. He explained everything to her.

Sure enough, I needed stitches. Thirteen of them, in fact—right under my chin. I notice the tender spot every time I shave, even now, decades later. This serves as a constant reminder of that day. The cut was caused by an accident and treated in an emergency room while a six-year-old version of me howled in pain.

Let's talk about our childhood scars, even the ones that did not have the chance to heal beautifully. You are most likely carrying the scars of your childhood. This could be a metaphor, of course, for any emotional damage that you have experienced. I will get to that in a few moments.

I have a scar on the top of my hand, where I cut myself in high school while working in a restaurant. I was grating Italian cheese when it happened, and it was a pretty bad cut. I said to the owner of the restaurant, "Hey, I just cut myself. I need to go to the hospital." He said, "WHAT…. the hospital? You cannot go to the hospital, that's ridiculous. Jump back in the kitchen and I will put a bandage on you."

Because of this man ordering me back to work, and me following his orders, there's a big scar on the back of my hand. I never went to the hospital and so, the injury was never graced by a surgeon's touch. Now, let's contrast that to times that I got my injuries treated: alongside the stitches I got on my chin at six years old, I've had surgeries on both my feet and had a hernia repair surgery earlier this year. It is interesting when a surgeon creates an incision and then carefully sews that incision up; although there sometimes may be a residual mar where a surgery took place, usually the skin comes out blemish-free. The skin on both of my feet is very smooth, and although there is a small scar, the surgeon took great care to make to minimize it—it's almost unnoticeable unless one inspects my feet closely.

How does a surgeon accomplish this? What is the difference between the work of a surgeon and the work of an emergency room physician?

The difference is that a surgeon is not rushed, he is not dealing with an emergency situation, and he can allow himself to be meticulous so that every cut is designed to heal in a way that hides the incision. It might not be perfect, and evidence might remain, but it's remarkable to see the results when it's not completed in a state of emergency.

This is a metaphor that I think is particularly useful to forgiveness. When we are injured emotionally, and it is untreated and left to heal on its own, it will mend slowly and often ineffectively. It will be exposed and leave a large scar. But when we use the process of forgiveness, an unrushed approach like that of a surgeon, the results leave minimal scarring. The skin is smooth, the cut is hidden, and the pain is not as obvious.

Four Minutes of Forgiveness:

Using the process detailed below will produce transformative results as if we have performed emotional surgery.

There are four elements and four actions within this process, and I call this the *Four Minutes of Forgiveness* exercise. You are already familiar with the idea of mindfulness and bringing your attention to the present moment. This exercise begins with paying attention to your present emotional pain, the persistent pain that you feel now that continues to linger and even grow.

Now when you are ready, close your eyes, perform your induction, and then focus on being present with the pain. Do not attach meaning to the pain, just observe the pain, the sadness, the grief, the loss, the fear, the other emotions that are related to the experience of pain that you feel in the present.

So many people believe that the pathway to emotional freedom is to eliminate negative pain. But research does not support that. It does not show that it's actually the best pathway. The best pathway for relieving emotional pain is to be present with the pain and just let a pain be a pain rather than ruminating on it.

The Self-Hypnosis Solution

By practicing this awareness, you create the ability to metaphorically place that pain on a leaf and let it simply float away, like in the *Leaves on the Stream* technique. Practice being present with your pain, and then move to a point of acceptance.

Now, acceptance does not mean that we like something, that we endorse it, that we're glad it happened, or that we hope it happens to other people. It does not mean that we believe that it was just. Acceptance simply means that we acknowledge that our pain and our past brought us to where we are today and that it's okay for us to move forward.

Forgiveness is the best road to releasing your emotional baggage. It is in this release that you can find meaning for your pain. This, of course, is reliant on your ability recognize forgiveness for its value.

In the Alcoholics Anonymous 12-Step program, participants recognize how their experiences can benefit other people. That does not mean that a former alcoholic commemorates alcoholism by sharing their own experience; it simply means that they have reached a point in their healing that they can pull meaning out of their struggles. I can find how my experiences can benefit other people. What do you value that leads you to forgive? You may forgive because you value love, joy, or equanimity. You can also create meaning out of your past struggles.

Although it might seem difficult to achieve, self-hypnosis can lead us to a trance state of forgiveness that gives us an ability to move to a mental point where just minutes ago we never thought we could reach. We can find emotional, physical, spiritual, and behavioral relief through the trance state of forgiveness. We can stop punishing ourselves. We can stop punishing others. We can live fully in the present moment.

I've named this the *Four Minutes of Forgiveness* because you can complete this exercise in four minutes—but it may take 40 four-minute sessions to build up to our first release and embark on the journey final release. That is okay. This is the great thing about self-hypnosis, it does not have to be rushed or performed perfectly, you will soon learn what pace and practices work best for you. By building your repertoire of gratitude, strategies, and value discoveries, you can pay more attention to the present moment and have greater levels of acceptance. You can increase your empathy and even extend it to those who we never thought we could have empathy for. The process itself is very powerful. Here is the full *Four Minutes of Forgiveness* process:

As always, you begin your session by removing all distractions, finding a comfortable place to sit or lay down, taking a few relaxing breaths, and performing your favorite self-hypnosis induction. Closing your eyes, take one minute to be present with your pain. Observe your pain. In earlier exercises, you observed your breath, now, observe your pain. What have you brought to the session because of the wrongs somebody has done to you? What pain have you brought to this time because you have not forgiven yourself for the mistakes that you've made?

In this first minute, what does that present pain look like? Does it look like low self-esteem? Does it look like sadness? Does it look like failure? Does it look like grief? Have you been open before to reflecting on what pains from the past still haunt you? Allow yourself to open yourself to them now, using your mindfulness skills. Now, simply say to yourself, "This is a grief, this is a sadness, this is a wrong, this is a hurt," and bring your attention back to the present, attending to this moment and neither ruminating in the past nor projecting into the future.

In the second minute, focus on the idea of acceptance. Acceptance, again, doesn't mean we endorse something. It does not mean that we hope that it happens to others. It doesn't even mean we're glad that it happened to us. Acceptance is simply acceptance. You can imagine those wrongs sitting on a table at an office, and you can see a box representing each one of those pains, whether it was self-inflicted or a product of others' transgressions. Acknowledge their presence. You neither have to hide from them nor pick them up off the table. Rather, when you're ready, you can simply turn, walk out the door of the office, turn the lights off, let those boxes exist where they are, and recognize that as you step forward, no matter how difficult the past is, you have an ability to experience gratitude.

What is it that you are grateful for? Today, I am grateful for my physical health. Today, I am grateful for my loving family. I'm grateful for my golden doodle. I am grateful that I have something to share with other people. Think for a minute. What is it that you can experience gratitude for? Repeat in your mind all that you are grateful for. Rather than paying attention to what you do not have, pay attention to what you do have. If you have chronic pain in your knee or hip, you can express your gratefulness like this: "I am grateful for the comfort I have in my shoulders. I'm grateful that my teeth don't ache."

After spending a minute in gratitude, we can put ourselves in a position of empathy. In empathy, you can see yourself accepting that other people are simply other people and that most perpetrators are actually victims, which does not justify the behaviors they engaged in but it explains what led them to wronging you. What values do you have?

Review the wrongs that have been done to you, or the wrongs that you have done to yourself. What meaning can you make of all of this madness? Can you visualize yourself benefiting others? Maybe you can do that through formal volunteer efforts, educating other people, or sharing with somebody else who you know is wounded and showing them a pathway to forgiveness through self-hypnosis.

In this last minute, you can take a breath and evaluate your emotions once again. Perhaps there is a newfound sense of relief or a sense of sadness, a sense of joy or a sense of magnified gratitude. Rather than judging it or following it, be present with it. Take another breath and open your eyes. By being present in this moment, I have the opportunity then to move into acceptance again, empathy again, meaning again, and continue the process of personal growth that is afforded to me by the practice of self-hypnosis.

This Four Minutes of Forgiveness process is profound. It can change your life. It can accomplish what perhaps years of therapy has been unable to accomplish. I share this technique with you because it's a technique that was helpful in my own life, and it's a technique that's been helpful in the lives of the clients who I've worked with over the years, who never thought that they could be present with their pain, that they didn't have to stop it, that they could accept even the unacceptable, and that they could have empathy simply because people are also people.

The Self-Hypnosis Solution

These processes of attending to gratitude, reflecting on our values, and releasing emotions are powerful. This can be done in four minutes. The reason why I created the Four Minutes of Forgiveness is because, often, we are not ready for a 40-minute forgiveness session. We can achieve 40 minutes of forgiveness by doing this once every week for ten weeks, or once a day for ten days, integrating forgiveness into our daily activities.

As I mentioned earlier, there is no right or wrong way to implement self-hypnosis into your daily lifestyle. It is okay if it takes you eight minutes to do this or twelve minutes to do this, and it's also okay to take bite-sized pieces that you can emotionally handle. They say, "What's the best way to eat an elephant?" One bite at a time. This process lends itself to cultivating a lifestyle of forgiveness and a lifestyle of exemplifying your core values despite the fact any difficult experiences in our background. The other great thing about this process is that it really is not focused on the past; it's focused on your present moment. The reality is, the question for all of us is not, "Where did I come from?" or even, "Where am I going?" The real question for us is, "Who am I today?" This self-discovery process will free you.

Chapter Twelve:
Future Pace Your Outcomes

Up to this point in the book, I have really put an emphasis on the present. Sometimes when people hear me stress the value of the present moment, what they interpret my message to be is, "Eat, drink, and be merry, because tomorrow we may die." I want to make clear that that is not the overriding philosophy on staying in the present moment. The overriding philosophy on mindfulness and staying in the present moment is: This is the moment, the only moment we can actually affect or change. We can't go change the past. We do not know what the future is. And if we do change the outcome of events in the future, that work is going to take place in the present. The past, of course, is important to us; it brings us to where we are today. The future is going to be determined by the actions that we take today. The future is not something to be ignored, but we need to understand how we create future success by creating change in

101

the present moment. Self-hypnosis is about the idea of future pacing.

Different measures of time, looking into the future. We actually have the ability to create the future we desire through the actions we take today.

Hypnosis begins with the idea of mindfulness, focusing on today. It is today that you act on an intention. You can move into success tomorrow because you created a day today that reflected what is most important. Continue through your understanding of time. You create success a week from now by taking actions based on your intentions this week. You can create the year that you want by developing a habit out of basing your actions off of your intentions. So, the outcome of the future is actually predicated by today.

I do a lot of work with weight loss clients, and one of the suggestions that I always give them is to download the pedometer app onto their smartphone. Back in the day, I actually used to give my clients plastic pedometers that fit under your belt. But now I simply tell people before they leave my office to download onto their phone an app that will track their steps. There are a bunch of them out there that are actually pretty accurate.

As I mentioned in Chapter Eight, the suggestion I give them in their hypnosis session is that they will take more steps today than yesterday, more steps tomorrow than today. They will increase their steps each and every day, until they reach 10,000 steps per day. Now, that is a suggestion that presumes an intention: "My intention is to be healthy. My intention is to increase my physical activity. My intention is to care for myself." So, it's a suggestion predicated by the intention that my client expresses. They can act on that intention as they go about the tasks of the day, in this case, taking more steps today than yesterday and taking more steps tomorrow than today. They continue to increase their steps each and every day until they reach 10,000 steps a day. 10,000 isn't a magic number; it could be 8,000 steps, 11,000, or 9,000 steps a day as well. What this is presupposing is, that after one month, after one year, they will create a habit.

So you can kind of see how this all melts together. Now, in our self-hypnosis practice, you have the ability to practice mindfulness and to be fully present in the moment. We have already covered how to set intentions and activate those intentions.

Your Future Pacing self-hypnosis session should go something like this:

>*After you have done your induction, see yourself as you are today, right now. Go ahead and close your eyes. With your eyes closed, focus on the intention that you've set. Meditate, if you will, for a moment, on that intention. And as you focus on that intention, see yourself tomorrow taking action on and following through on that intention. See yourself in the scenarios and the situations where you will be, perhaps with other people, perhaps on your own, perhaps at work, or perhaps going about your business at home. See yourself as you know you will be tomorrow, because you have set this*

intention today. And ask yourself: What actions are the result of my intention?

Will I be more focused? Will I be more disciplined? Will I be more attentive? Will I be more assertive? Will I be more joyful? Will I be more intelligent? Will I be more compassionate? And see yourself. Create a vision in your mind of acting on that intention and imagine what tomorrow will bring as a result. As you continue to focus on that idea of what tomorrow will be, future pace out another week. And after a week of acting on the intentions, taking the actions you know that will bring you to that highest level of peak performance: sharing genuinely, manifesting compassion towards others, sharing joys with people, forgiving yourself. See yourself as you know you will be a week from now.

Bring yourself out a year from now or a decade from now. See yourself as you know you will be, not because we can determine the future with our mind, but because we've determined the present with our mind. See yourself a year from now, having cultivated a habit based on actions that are in alignment with your intention. Notice how it feels. Notice what you're doing. Notice what the results have been for you.

Take however much time you desire to visualize and enjoy your future events, journeys, and experiences. Once you are ready, bring yourself back to your present consciousness.

What we can create with our mind, we can experience in real life. I have confidence that your tomorrow, your next week, and your next year are going to be aligned with the tools of self-hypnosis and good success. You've not only learned something new, but you've cultivated a habit—a habit of living hypnotically, based on practicing the things that you've learned with the intention of living your best life.

Over the next week, as you practice your self-hypnosis, practice with an open mind—not only mindfully paying attention to the moment, but future pacing your success for your health, your wealth, and your habits. Enter tomorrow, next week, and next year knowing that what you've created today will shape your future.

Future Pacing Session Example:

> *As always, begin by removing the typical distractions, settle into your space, and begin your favorite self-hypnosis induction.*
>
> *Take a breath. Allow that breath to fill your lungs with oxygen, to bring you a sense of wellbeing and energy. It feels great to create a visualization of your future self, based on your present experience of acting with intention.*
>
> *Take in another breath. Stretch out the muscles that need to be stretched. Relax your shoulders. Move your neck. Breathe in another breath, just noticing the power of this moment to create your ideal future. And when you're ready, open your eyes with a smile on your face, feeling fantastic and ready for the rest of the day.*

This future pacing technique is a technique involving visualization of the future, but it is all predicated on our intentions in the moment. Practice this as you practice your self-hypnosis techniques. In fact, you might really be enjoying the experiences you are creating of seeing yourself as you know you will be. Why? Because of your intentions today, your actions tomorrow, and your habits between now and next year.

Enjoy the visualizations you create. Enjoy contemplating the outcomes for growth that it will create. Embrace the process of self-hypnosis in a way that truly helps you to elevate your higher self and to set aside anything, either known or unknown, which had up to this point held you back from success in any area of life.

Chapter Thirteen:
The 20-Minute Mirror Technique

This self-hypnosis technique comes from Milton Erickson. It is a strategy that is unlike any I've taught so far, and as a matter of fact, it'll be the easiest to perform. It has the potential for the most profound results.

The chair I'm sitting in as I write this book is one I purchased 15 years ago for my hypnosis clinic. Over the last decade and a half, many clients have sat in this exact chair and experienced profoundly. I've helped people to overcome a fear of flying. I've helped people deal with depression and grief. I've helped people control anxiety. I've helped people quit smoking. And I have taught many people the methods of self-hypnosis as they sat in this very chair.

This chair intentionally faces a large mirror. This is a self-hypnosis technique that's really profound and there are many occasions when I've sat in this chair and used this technique myself.

In your quiet spot, position a comfortable chair directly in front of a large mirror. Set a timer for 20 minutes. As you sit in your chair, seeing yourself in the mirror, simply allow yourself to experience the trance state that is most resourceful for you. There really are no other directions.

Erickson was a medical hypnotherapist. He worked as a therapist and a psychiatrist from the 1950s into the 1980s. Many consider him the father of modern medical hypnosis.

Back in the 1950s a woman contacted him and said, "After I first saw you, hypnosis was so helpful. I bought a book on self-hypnosis but I've spent hours trying to practice the techniques and the principles in this book and I haven't had the same results that I had when I was with you."

Dr. Erickson explained to her that her lack of success was because the idea expressed in the book was that you would take something from outside of yourself and program it into your unconscious or subconscious mind. It was predicated that our subconscious mind, sometimes referred to as our higher self, has infinite wisdom. It knows what we need.

His instructions to her were to simply sit in a chair in front of a mirror and to set a timer for 20 minutes. She said that her first experience doing this, she thought there must be something wrong because as soon as she sat down, the timer went off. She took great care setting it again. Again, much to her surprise, the timer went off. She looked at the clock to check, and in fact, 20 minutes had passed.

The results of this process can be life changing! Our subconscious mind, our higher self, is filled with wisdom. We actually do possess all of the problem-solving resources within us at any time, even if it doesn't feel like it right now. Instead of looking outside for your experience, you should look inward and pull something out to add to your experience.

Here is the process again: Simply sit in a comfortable chair across from a mirror large enough to see your full physical self. Set a timer for 20 minutes. Gaze at yourself. Attend to yourself. Be present with yourself without judgment, without hurry, without doing anything special, and listen to your own inner guide. Listen to your higher self. Access the subconscious resources within you that you can bring to any situation that you face today. That's it. Nothing more, nothing less. The results, without a doubt, will be profound in every aspect of your life.

Chapter Fourteen:
It Works!

In 1926, Roy Herbert Jarrett wrote *It Works*. It really was not even a book; it was a very short pamphlet that shared a technique. He never referred to it as a "hypnotic" technique, but it is in fact a very effective and time proven self-hypnosis technique. Millions of copies were distributed, within the first couple of years. And of course, over the last almost 100 years, millions of people have benefited from the contribution that Mr. Jarrett made to understanding how to achieve our dreams.

So far, we've covered a lot of different things: the physical aspects of progressive muscle relaxation and autogenic training; we've talked about mindfulness and putting some space between you and your thoughts; I've shared a number of different techniques to help you address the metaphysical or spiritual issues that are important to you, such as forgiveness. Now, in this chapter, I will share a self-hypnosis technique that can help you to acquire anything you truly desire. Now, it might seem phenomenal that I promise that, with self-hypnosis, you can achieve or gain anything that you want. But what I have discovered in my own life is that when we practice principles like those offered by Mr. Jarrett, we reap the fruits of those efforts.

2015 was a particularly difficult time in my life; I wasn't in the best of health, I had multiple surgeries, and things really were not going my way. I lost my voice for a period of time. I could not speak at all. I had multiple throat surgeries, and I was bummed out. I was very depressed and could not see any real future for myself.

In an effort to pull myself out of the funk that had overtaken my life, I did what many people often talk about: I created a vision board. At that time, I did not have the energy to actually cut pictures from magazines and make a collage on a poster board. Instead, I just went to Google Images and created a digital version that I could look at on my screen. I also made it so I could print it out on a regular eight-and-a-half by eleven piece of paper.

I was looking at those pictures, those representations of the things that I truly wanted. Even though it was a difficult year for me, the reality was that by the end of the year, I looked up one day and realized I possessed all that was on my vision board. When I first put the pictures on the collage, it did not even feel attainable. But, by the end of the year, the unlimited potential of programming my subconscious mind came to fruition.

The Self-Hypnosis Solution

I then learned about *It Works*, and I've since changed my method. Over the last couple of years, I've been using this method in self-hypnosis to truly achieve what's most important to me. Rather than pictures on a board, I use a small notebook. For you to do this as well, you will need a small notebook or at least multiple pieces of paper.

One of our biggest problems in life is that we often don't evaluate what we truly want. We have fleeting ideas, but we don't materialize them, we don't write them down. In fact, many people focus more on what they don't want rather than what they do want! There is something powerful about your own handwriting staring back at you. It becomes a self-confrontation. It takes a thought and makes it tangible.

The process begins with taking a piece of paper of the first page of the notebook and writing down seven to ten things that you truly want. By the way, this is not the time to be completely and totally altruistic and write "I want global world peace." World peace might be one of your wishes, but this is the time for you to really identify what you want personally.

Do you want to drive a Maybach? Do you want $10,000 a month in salary? Do you want your own pickleball court in your backyard? Do you want a fulfilling relationship? What is it that you truly want? Write them down.

Sometimes, the process of defining what we want produces some changes. Each and every day, revisit that list of wants. Aim to take some of those things off the list within the first week and then replace them with new entries. This is really about homing in on what's truly most important to us.

By the end of seven to ten days, you will have a well-developed, well thought out list. Each and every day, spend three minutes, three times a day, reading the list to yourself. "I want a Maybach. I want $10,000 a month. I want a committed marriage with a beautiful spouse. I want to finish a book I've been working on. I want another golden doodle puppy." Spend three minutes, three times a day looking at your list, focusing on the list.

We don't necessarily need to worry about how we're going to achieve those things, but we should be creating a plan. Dr. Jarrett actually gives us three steps that we need to take in order to actualize our desires.

1. We need to make a written list of the things that we desire in the order of importance. We've already discussed how to go about doing that. Do not be afraid to put too many things on your list. It's important to review that list over a period of a few days and to be bold; add the desires that truly exist inside of your heart. You can add in details, color, size, location, all of those sorts of things.

2. Begin manifesting those things by each day, three times a day, spending at least three minutes reviewing the list. Think about the things on your list as often as possible throughout the day.

3. Do not discuss the items on this list with anyone. The reason is simple: You want the manifestation of your desires to

come from within. And by discussing this with other people, you might come to the conclusion that someone else handed you what you wanted rather than you working towards it. And so, as these wishes manifest in your life, you can cross them off the list and recognize that it was from within you that all of them came to fruition. This is a powerful process that can help you to make tremendous amounts of change.

You may alter your list by either adding items as your priorities shift or removing them as you attain them or as you decide they are no longer quite important to you.

While you should not talk about the contents of your list to anyone, you might benefit from associating with those who have what you strive for. This is an important element of activating our wildest dreams into reality. They, whoever they are, say that our average salary is the average of our five closest friends. Birds of a feather flock together.

Dr. Jarrett's method of focusing on a list, adding to the list what is important to us, removing what becomes unimportant, refining the list, and defining the list in specific detail activates within us a higher self, a greater consciousness to the steps and the tasks that will lead us into success.

By using this as a method of activating our greatest level of potential in self-hypnosis, we can discover true success at an unlimited level.

Chapter Fifteen:
Hands as Thoughts

A self-hypnosis idea that comes from acceptance and commitment therapy is seeing our hands as our thoughts. This was written by Russ Harris (2009) in the book *ACT Made Simple*. It's a strategy that I've used to help clients whom I've taught self-hypnosis; it helps them to really understand how their thoughts are simply a part of their experience—something that can be observed. It's very tactile and kinesthetic and I love kinesthetic processes in self-hypnosis because we not only get to be hypnotized, but we also get to *feel* hypnotized.

Think back to our autogenic training, where you created the sensation of warmth or heaviness in your hands. This process begins by simply holding out the hands as if they are a book and examining your hands as if they are your thoughts. Imagine that your thoughts are extended from you. Your thoughts are in front of you. They can be observed.

Now place your hands over your face, over your eyes and touching your nose. Notice that there are gaps. There are gaps between your fingers. You can feel the hand touching your nose. You can feel your hands touching your face, but you can see between those gaps. These are your thoughts that are often obscuring your viewpoint and keeping you from seeing the bigger picture. This metaphor is a useful tool in self-hypnosis. You can bring your hands to your face and you can observe through your hands and ask yourself, "What thoughts keep going through my mind that are keeping me from being able to see everything in the world around me that is important to me?"

Look through the gaps of your fingers. What's in view? What is restricted? What is clear? If you were to go about the tasks of the day with your hands in front of your face, what would you miss? What would you be unable to do? What would be the consequences of making that choice? By engaging in this process, it helps us see how sometimes our own thoughts inhibit us from being able to function at our highest level. Spend a couple of moments to clarify your thoughts and, once you remove your hands, ask yourself, "What are the things I value most? What is most important to me? What action can I take now that would be beneficial to me and to others in the world around me?

By engaging in these tasks and actions, you have clarified your thoughts using self-hypnosis and a practical exercise.

Chapter Sixteen:
Cultivating the Observer Self

Here is something profound: If you can notice something, you cannot actually be that something. In other words, if you can notice a part of you that is depressed, you cannot actually be that depression. This is how we put some space between us and negative energy, or between us and our thoughts. This is, if you will, another mindfulness exercise, and it's a great tool for self-hypnosis.

Self-hypnosis is really about creating an increase in awareness. We are increasing our awareness that we are not our thoughts or our feelings. We are an observer of our thoughts, our feelings, and our sensations. By being an observer, we can put some space between us and the objects of our observation. This process can be done after a short hypnosis induction. You can bring yourself to the resourceful state that we call hypnosis using any of the induction methods which have previously been discussed.

With your eyes closed, pay attention to your breathing and, as you breathe the air in, notice the air that you inhale is cooler than the air that you exhale. Do you notice that? Pay attention again. Breathe in the air, and notice that it is cooler than the air that you exhale. Notice something about noticing that—that there is a part of you that notices. This is the observer. In self-hypnosis, the observer can become a very important resource for us.

Pay attention in this moment to your thoughts. What is it that you are thinking? Are you thinking about this process, about self-hypnosis, about learning new things? Are you thinking about the tasks that must be done this afternoon, or when your next meeting is? Notice that there is a part of you that notices these thoughts. Thoughts are something that can be observed, which means that we actually are not our thoughts.

Pay attention to your physical sensation, your experience of being right now. Is there pressure? Is there pain? Is there comfort? Is there softness? What is it you notice about your physical state? Observe that. Observe what you notice and notice again there's a part of you that has the ability to be an observer to notice these things. Self-hypnosis really is about increasing our awareness.

As you relax into this moment, what images are in your mind? What pictures do you see? Do you observe you watching yourself as you engage in this process of self-hypnosis? Do you see something creative that you have created with your imagination? Can you observe that and, once again, can you notice that part of you that has the ability to notice these things?

Pay attention to the room around you, to my voice, to the sounds that you hear, the wind outside, the air-conditioning or heating vent overhead, the background noises from outside of your window. What is it that you can observe right now about what it is that you can hear? As you observe these things with your ears, notice that there's a part of you that has the ability to notice these things, to become aware of these things.

Any emotions that you experience right now, you can also observe: a comfort, a discomfort, an anxiety, a fear, a happiness, a joy. Pay attention to the emotions that you feel right now. Become an observer of those feelings and notice that there is a part of you who has the ability to notice these things.

Let me ask you a question now: Who is doing the noticing? You are doing the noticing. There is a part of you that notices. That is what we call the observer self, and, in a self-hypnosis experience, we have the ability to be both the person who experiences as well as the person who observes. When our self-hypnosis practice is over, we have the ability to put some space between us and our thoughts, our feelings, our emotions, our senses, ourselves, and other people, by becoming an observer of the experiences we have.

By being an observer, you remain fully in the present moment. You set aside any rumination or regrets of the past or fears of the future. You allow yourself to move into a new pattern of behavior where you observe before you act, reducing impulsivity. By observing, you have the ability to see yourself from a new vantage point, one from outside of yourself. This permit us to experience the world around us in a new way. While we can accomplish this practice in a self-hypnosis experience like this, we also have the ability to take this skill into our real world on an everyday basis.

Go ahead and open your eyes now. Notice the smile on your face. A part of you has the ability to both create that and a part of you has the ability to notice that. It feels pretty good to have a smile on your face right now, doesn't it? You can always put some space between you and the world around you, to act with intention, to act without impulsivity, and to act in a way that not only serves you best, but serves your family, your community, and the world around you.

A practical application of this is in social media. I notice that many of my very well-intentioned friends often post without thinking, without putting some space between them and their thoughts or them and their observations. The observer self helps us create empathy and to see new perspectives, to become more psychologically flexible. In the social media posts that I read, I often see people who have a lack of psychological flexibility; they rant and rave about things they have no control over. Most often, they do this because they have not put any space between them and their observations. They have not noticed the part of them that has the capacity to notice. This exercise is helps us to not only be a better person, but to get along with others in the world in a new and beneficial way.

This exercise comes from ACT Therapy, Acceptance and Commitment Therapy. It's a very useful training tool for psychotherapy clients, who often become their depression or become their anxiety or become their pain rather than an observer of those elements. My weight loss clients become their hunger rather than an observer of their hunger. My cigarette smoking clients become their withdrawal rather than an observer of their withdrawal. By practicing the observer perspective, we can help ourselves in self-hypnosis to make our real world a better place.

Chapter Seventeen:
The New Behavior Generator

"I can do this, I can do this, I can do this!" Have you ever wanted to change your behavior, or more specifically, actually start doing something that would be valuable or resourceful to you? Is it changing your eating patterns? Is it doing your yard work?

I am notorious for having the second worst yard on my block. I never want to be the worst yard in the neighborhood, I have just never been a big fan of doing yard work before. I actually have no problem being the second worst yard in the neighborhood: I don't get all the negative attention and I don't have to expend energy to make my yard look nice.

Last year I bought a new house. When I bought the new house, I decided that I was going to, after 50 some years, finally break the mold of having the second worst yard in the neighborhood and take care of my yard. I bought a hedge trimmer. I bought a weed eater. I bought some buckets to pick up debris. I bought a blower. I bought a big broom. I bought all the accoutrements that I would need to be able to take care of my yard and perhaps be able to bump myself up to owner of the best yard in the neighborhood.

Even though that was my intention when I moved in, I noticed after a few months of living there that I had, once again, returned to my old title of owner of the second worst yard in the neighborhood.

So, what I did was the self-hypnosis technique called a **New Behavior Generator.** It is amazing! Whatever new behavior you would like to generate, you can use this strategy to do so. It will program you to not only act on the behavior, but to actually make it a habit.

Yesterday, when I was driving back from the park with the kids and our golden doodle, I pulled into my driveway and I looked at my yard. For the first time in as long as I can remember, I was proud of my yard, realizing that my yard was actually way better than most of my neighbors' yards. It looked so good. And that was because I have been going out there on a regular basis and taking care of my yard.

How does this new behavior generator work? How does one break an old pattern such as neglecting one's yard work and establish a new pattern? It is easy. Simply close your eyes and access your resourceful state of self-hypnosis. And in that resource state of self-hypnosis, focus on what you truly want to do. In my case, I wanted to make my yard look as good as I possibly could, to make it stand out, to make it something I could be proud of. I envisioned in my mind the end result of my efforts.

In my self-hypnosis, after creating a mental 8 x 10 glossy image of my yard being beautiful, I decided to expand that imagery into the scene of a movie. The kind of place where a Hollywood film scout might come and say, "We need a front yard of an average American neighborhood and we'd love it if we could use your front yard." And so, I imagined my front yard being in a movie, and I imagined myself making a movie, a documentary of me taking care of my yard in order to make it good enough for a Hollywood movie. And so, I created a movie in my mind of me trimming the hedges; I created a movie of me sweeping the walkways; I created a movie of me using the blower to remove debris from underneath the bushes in my yard.

I played these movie clips over and over, and gradually amplified the details of each—imagining the sound of the blower, the green of the well-watered leaves, the sound of me using the trimmers to trim the tree. All of these things were elements of my movie. I enjoyed playing that movie and I amplified and I paid attention to each of the attributes of me doing the work: I paid attention to the feeling of exercise—it's a good feeling; I paid attention to the feeling of sweat; I paid attention to the feeling of the sun and the vitamin D that was helping my body and my immune system become even stronger. I really focused on all of the elements of putting together a complete cinematic compilation of the new behavior that I wanted to engage in.

What I did then is I put myself in three scenarios where I saw myself in that movie doing my yard work before a holiday weekend. I always appreciated in the past when my neighbors before the holiday weekend, Memorial Day, Labor Day, 4th of July, and Thanksgiving would make an effort to make their home look really nice. So I pictured myself noticing an impending holiday on the calendar and getting ready to make my yard look really nice. I then viewed myself in another scenario where yard work needed to be done after having a lot of wind during the windy season or rain during the rainy season, when the yard can become dirty and muddy and outside debris could be blown onto it. I saw myself cleaning up the mess that needed to be cleaned up following a storm, putting myself in that mental movie.

The third time, of course, is when the Hollywood producers came and said, "We'd like to feature your yard in a movie. Would you be willing to clean it up and make it look really nice so that we can use it for a Hollywood movie shoot?" So, I pictured myself in that third scenario, getting ready to have my yard star in a Hollywood movie. And in self-hypnosis, I spent a day or two mentally rehearsing these scenes, these new behaviors in my mind. And guess what? The result has been that over the last several months I've consistently had what I think is probably one of the best yards in the neighborhood. It was interesting. I was just out talking to my neighbor the other day and he said, "Your yard always looks so nice." And I thought to myself, thank goodness I know the new behavior generator because I've set aside my old pattern of having the second worst yard in the neighborhood and now, I have, without a doubt, one of the best yards in the neighborhood.

You can use this new behavior generator yourself. What behavior would you like to generate? Would you like to see yourself setting aside a portion of your paycheck each week and saving a hundred dollars in a savings account? Would you like to see yourself manicuring your nails rather than biting them? Would you like to see yourself responding with empathy and kindness rather than anger? This new behavior generator can be utilized literally with any behavior that you would like to create, but more importantly, that you would like to create an ongoing response to.

The process really is pretty simple: Close your eyes and create a mental picture, an 8 x 10 glossy photo, of the outcome that's important for you. See yourself in that image with the success that is important to you. Amplify that picture into a movie, it might only be a two or three minute movie, perhaps a movie of you going through the drive through window and depositing that paycheck but putting one hundred dollars into your savings account, and then coming home to log onto your online bank account and seeing your balance increase each and every week.

Next, create that mental movie, whatever it is, and amplify the aspects of the movie that make it real for you. Turn up the volume, make the color brighter, sharper, crisper, clearer. Pay attention to the aspects of it. Is the image far, or is the image near? And allow yourself to associate fully into this image and see yourself doing the tasks in this movie that are important to you. And then see yourself in three different scenarios, generating and using this new behavior. Taking a breath, allow yourself to feel awesome, knowing that what the mind can conceive, the body can achieve. Take in another breath. If your eyes aren't open, open them with a smile on your face, feeling fantastic, knowing that the new behavior generator is a powerful way for you to embrace success and to live your best life.

In the sample of saving money, see yourself saving money prior to purchasing something important. See yourself in a scenario where you have saved money over a long enough period of time, and the result is you now can create a better life for yourself doing the things that you want to do. In your movie, create a scenario where you are doing the task of saving money and the result is something important or meaningful for you.

It's pretty cool to be able to create that new behavior and to see it in your mind. Perhaps the issue was getting a manicure and maintaining beautiful fingernails rather than biting them off. See yourself out for dinner, passing a plate, and somebody else noticing your beautiful nails. See yourself typing on your keyboard with your nails manicured and clean. See yourself in the third scenario, a third situation, where your nails are the way you would finally like to be them. Generate the new behavior of manicuring your nails and taking care of them on a regular basis, rather than sporadically.

You can create any example, any scenario, any new behavior that would be useful to you. See yourself in three different scenarios or three different situations, manifesting that which you have created. And because we have the ability to use the creative mind to put ourselves into scenarios that we create, we have the ability to experience this in reality. Anything that exists in our physical world had to be a thought first.

You have generated this new behavior here in self-hypnosis. You have applied it in three different ways to three different scenarios. I have no doubt that by spending some time between now and next week, practicing the new behavior generator as an aspect of your self-hypnosis practice, you will discover that it is easy for you to manifest this, not only in the creative mind, but in your real world as well.

Chapter Eighteen:
Self-Hypnosis for Pain Control

There are literally thousands of articles in peer reviewed journals—in fact, over 12,000 of them—that show hypnosis as a viable pathway to help people experience success, to help people recover faster from medical conditions, to help people establish new behaviors and rise into a state of excellence.

In this chapter I want to focus on the one area of hypnosis that undoubtedly has more evidence than anything else, and that is the area of pain control. Hypnosis and self-hypnosis are excellent strategies for dealing with chronic and ongoing pain.

Now, of course, if one experiences a new pain or an acute pain, one should always seek out treatment from a licensed medical professional. The reality is, though, many of us experience ongoing chronic pain. We had been seen by a physician. They understand the nature and the cause of the pain. They perhaps prescribed various treatments to us, probably including meditation, maybe some stretching, or other tools like that. By adding self-hypnosis to your repertoire of strategies, you are going to be able to discover relief from the chronic painful conditions which cause you difficulty in life.

I came to the field of hypnosis early on as a result of chronic pain. I was in an automobile accident when I was 18 years old. I went to see a chiropractor. Of course, I was 18, I did not have any insurance and he agreed to see me for a reduced fee. But more importantly than that, he and I struck up a friendship of sorts and he became a tremendous mentor to me. He asked me if I would facilitate his Thursday night pain control group, which really consisted him of teaching self-hypnosis techniques to his clients. So, I began to facilitate that group with him. That was one of my earliest experiences with hypnosis, and the patients who came to that group found relief, just as when I applied the same techniques in my own life I also found relief from chronic pain.

In my adult years, I've suffered from various forms of arthritis. In fact, I have had numerous foot surgeries over the past few years. Those are the results of bone degeneration and inflammation in the joints; self-hypnosis has been a particularly great tool in alleviating my pain. Now, somebody once said to me, "Well, if you're such a great hypnotist, why did you end up having surgery?" The reality is because I'm a great hypnotist, I ended up having surgery. In other words, I was so efficient at managing my pain levels that when a normal person had progressed to the point where I had, they would have been screaming at the top of their lungs for intervention, but I wasn't. I was managing it well, and the result was that the degeneration in the joints in my feet got to a point where the only answer was a fusion.

The result of the fusion is that it instantly decreased my pain. In fact, it eliminated my pain in those joints because the joints no longer existed. Unfortunately that was soon replaced with discomfort, with what I now really understand is sort of a form of phantom limb pain. In other words, my brain has been telling my foot for the last 54 years, move, automatically, subconsciously. It isn't something that I have to consciously think of. We move our feet; we adjust our toes all day long. But because I have a fusion and because there's screws holding those fusions into place, my feet don't move like they used to.

The result of that is kind of interesting. My brain is still sending that signal to my feet, to move in those certain ways, and that becomes emotionally distressing. It becomes painful, which is intriguing from a physical perspective, seeing as there is no joint there. The pain is clearly a faulty signal between my foot and my brain. Self-hypnosis is a wonderful tool for dealing with any type of chronic or ongoing pain. Whether we are dealing with migraine headaches, orthopedic-related issues, as well as the emotional pain that sometimes accompanies the physical feelings, self-hypnosis can be you answer

The technique of mindfulness that we have already focused on in this book is an effective strategy in and of itself. There are literally thousands of articles, just as there are thousands of articles showing the efficacy of hypnosis, showing the efficacy of mindfulness meditation techniques. I view all of these techniques as forms of self-hypnosis. They are hypnotic strategies that are sufficient to create a reduction and even an elimination in the pain that people experience. The reason why is simple: mindfulness puts space between you and your pain. Rather than your pain being you, your pain is something that you simply notice. By putting some space between you and your pain, your pain can just be a pain without it meaning something to you. It is often the meaning of our pain that causes us the most distress.

I've shared with you what researchers have vetted a tremendous method for pain management, the 3-2-1 Reset technique, or any other technique that focuses on the idea of mindfulness; paying attention to this moment; not judging our thoughts, our sensations, our feelings. Those are all strategies that are truly useful for those who deal with chronic pain.

I want to share with you now four specific strategies that we can incorporate into our self-hypnosis.

After we do our hypnotic induction, again, the question is what comes next. These are four different processes that you can utilize in your self-hypnosis to help you deal with chronic pain. Many times people have an all-or-none mindset: "I either have pain or I don't have it." They think that having pain is bad and having no pain is good; It's going to be either one or the other. While it may be true that many people experience pain elimination when they practice these techniques, the majority of cases result in a reduction in pain.

A reduction in pain is also a success. If your pain is keeping you from being able to go to work, get out of bed, to have joy in your life, assess if you would be able to engage in these things if you reduced that pain by 10%, or by 15%, or by 20%. Can I now bring a smile to my face even if I don't yet feel joy? How about 40% or 50%, does that make a difference in my quality of life? The answer to that is yes. By employing these techniques, you'll have a variety of different levels of success. One technique might be more useful than another technique. If you're new to pain control and self-hypnosis, I would suggest practicing not only mindfulness and mastering the art of mindfulness, but also these four techniques. By practicing these four techniques, you'll be able to decide which one or two are most effective for you.

To begin, the easiest thing to do is to access the state of self-hypnosis: You can use the 3-2-1 Reset; you can use the 4-6-8 method; you can use the Contextual Skill-Building Induction; you can use any type of induction that you prefer. Close your eyes and bring yourself to that resourceful state that we call hypnosis.

The first technique that we are going to utilize is called **Dissociation.** We are going to dissociate from our pain. So often, our pain is integrated into who we are while we're experiencing it. By spending some time practicing the mental art of dissociation, we can put some space between us and our pain, just like we can with mindfulness. Using the imaginative faculties of our mind, we can use a creative process to engage in dissociation and to essentially take the pain from our body and let it rest next to us.

So with your eyes closed, as you breathe in and breathe out, imagine your body is a Lego set. Imagine a plastic Lego head. Imagine plastic Lego arms, plastic Lego shoulders, a plastic Lego torso, a plastic Lego rear end, plastic Lego legs, and plastic Lego feet. With Legos, you can, with force, remove one of the blocks. So by imagining your body as if it is a body made out of Legos, you can actually imagine being able to remove the bricks that hurt. Imagine taking out one or two or three or four of the bricks in the place where you're experiencing pain and imagine setting those bricks on the floor next to the chair, where you sit.

Pay attention to the bricks that remain, the rest of you, the part of you that is in this chair and notice how comfortable it feels to have set those Lego bricks of pain off to the side. As the pain sits next to you, imagine that the pain inside of those removed bricks is less intense. What you've done here is you've allowed yourself to reduce the awareness of pain, paying attention to your comfort in this moment, and it feels pretty good, doesn't it? Take a couple of more moments to simply enjoy this feeling of comfort with those Lego bricks of pain removed.

Now imagine that as those Lego bricks of pain sit in the chair next to you, without a connection to the rest of your body, the power of that pain simply disappears from those bricks. It's pretty fun to recognize that we have such a creative imagination and that we can imagine that. When you're ready, when you've paid attention to your comfort, imagine picking up those bricks you set off to the side and carefully plugging them back in, noticing that as they join with the rest of the comfortable you, they transform into a source of comfort themselves rather than a source of pain. Feels pretty good to dissociate from our pain, to separate ourselves from our pain.

The second technique actually adds to the Disassociation technique, and it's called **Sensory Splitting.** In sensory splitting, we focus on the pain. Imagine that part of the body where you've been experiencing chronic pain. Let the images of the Lego bricks disappear for a moment and return your awareness back to your normal everyday body. Pay attention to the place where you have felt pain. What does this pain feel like? Does it throb? Or, does it stick? Is it a burning sensation? Is it a poking sensation? Is it an oppressing sensation? Is the pain dull or is the pain sharp?

Pay attention to this sensation and notice how you can pay attention to the dullness, or the sharpness, or the burning. Without paying attention to the pain, you've split the symptom from the pain. When you notice that feeling of heat, or poking, or sharpness, or throbbing, imagine being able to turn a dial to reduce the intensity of that sensation. Reduce it by 20%, and now by 40%, and now by 60%, and even all the way down, turning off the throbbing, the poking, the sticking.

Notice that in the spot where you split the sensation from the pain, any pain that remains is not pain that has importance because the distressing symptom is something you've split and removed from your experience. Feels pretty good, doesn't it, to be able to use this strategy, to notice something and explore your body right now? Notice the feeling of comfort and the absence of distressful pain. Notice that the comfort is in the present moment, and at this point it's almost as if you've forgotten to remember the pain at all.

The next strategy that we can use is a strategy called ***Age Regression*** or ***Age Progression***. This is an ability in self-hypnosis to imagine ourselves either as we were before or as we know we can be in the future. In Age Regression, allow yourself to continue to relax into this moment and think of a time before that pain ever existed; maybe it was before an injury or an accident, or before you had an awareness of the pain that's caused you distress. Think of a time before that pain ever existed. It feels pretty good to recall how wonderful our bodies felt at one point, because we're able to revivify our previous experiences. One of the things we have the ability to do is to act on the resourceful state that already exists within our body of comfort rather than pain. So as you roll out the tasks of the day, act as if you are experiencing your body in a time that preceded the current distress. You'll notice that throughout the day, you'll find comfort where before we experienced pain.

You can, of course, use Age Progression to see yourself as you know you can be in the future. You can do this because you're learning self-hypnosis, because you're applying these principles, and because you've practiced the various methods of induction and mindfulness that I've taught you in this book. You can have confidence that a week from now, a month from now, or a year from now, as your body heals and your mind expands, you can actualize the vision of how you see yourself as you know you will be. You will see yourself without the distress of the pain, which has caused you so much difficulty. Of course, anything we can create with the mind, we can experience with our reality. So, we must utilize our ability to think of the future right now. So, check your present experience and notice how comfortable it feels to be as if there is no pain.

Our fourth strategy that we can use, is called ***Symbolic Imagery***. Imagine your pain as something else, perhaps an irritating sound, a bothersome light, or even something random like a power tool, a machine, or an irritating orange traffic cone. When you think of your pain, you think of something out there that is irritating or difficult or unappealing. What is it that you're thinking of? Imagine your pain as that object. Imagine your pain as that orange traffic cone. Imagine your pain as theater lights shining into your eyes. Imagine your pain with some other creative symbolic representation. It is amazing how creative our minds are and how easy it is for you to do that.

Pay attention with your mind's eye to the object you have created, to the irritating characteristics of it. If it's light, dim the lights or point the lights in the other direction. If it is a color, change the color of that orange traffic cone to a soothing blue. Or if it is an irritating sound, change the sound coming out of that leaf blower in your neighbor's yard to, perhaps, the sound of relaxing music. Now imagine that instead of this object being right in front of your face, it moves back, putting some distance between you and it.

The Self-Hypnosis Solution

You will notice that reducing the irritation represented by that object simultaneously reduces the physical experience of your current pain. Continue to amplify your ability to reduce the irritation of that device, that object, or that symbol. Notice how good your body feels: notice a sense of wellness, a sense of health, a sense of strength where pain was once present.

All four of these strategies can be used and mentally rehearsed as a process to alleviate your chronic pain. Your assignment? Over the next day or two, the next week or two, the next month or two, practice these techniques of hypnotic pain control in your self-hypnosis, discovering that with each and every day, in each and every way, you get better and better.

Now, enjoy the relief you have created. Enjoy the experience of comfort. Enjoy living your best life even with the difficulties life brings us sometimes.

Chapter Nineteen:
The Promises of Self-Hypnosis

Self-hypnosis is a powerful tool. After reading about the techniques I have shared in this book, it is easy to hypnotize yourself and easy to benefit from it. These techniques will take your practice the to next level. In my first book, *The Seven Most Effective Methods of Self Hypnosis: How to Create Rapid Change in Your Health, Wealth, and Habits,* I laid a foundation for the methods of self-induction. In this book, I have added new methods (The 3-2-1 Reset Technique and others) and I have gone deeper into answering the question of, "What now?"

The ideas in this book have been designed to be an easy to follow guide that will yield specific results. The promise of self-hypnosis is that by applying the principles in this book you will know how to create physical calm and emotional serenity. But it goes deeper than that. When you master the ideas in this book and practice self-hypnosis you will discover a more powerful version of yourself, one who will intuitively handle situations in new ways. You will have broken old lifelong patterns that have not been resourceful and replaced them with new actionable plans for the future.

By living with intention today rather than striving for something in the future you harness the power of now. In my own life I used to be crippled by anxiety, I suffered from self-doubt, I was paralyzed by resentment and fear. Self-hypnosis has been a pathway to making real changes for me. In my job as a hypnotist I have tried to share these ideas with others, and the results have been amazing.

I have seen clients overcome emotional blocks, act with emotional intelligence, and step into abundance. I have seen clients stop smoking, lose weight, and make behavioral changes. But for me, the most powerful observation has been seeing clients who develop a daily practice of self-hypnosis become confident, powerful, and full of joy.

I want to encourage you to practice the techniques in this book. The real power of self-hypnosis comes not by trying these techniques out a few times, but through the repetition of a daily practice. Commit to spending 21 days practicing the Contextual Skill-Building induction and commit to practicing the 30201 Reset Technique on a daily basis. At first you might not notice much, but with daily practice comes subtle and significant growth and soon you will come to a magnificent realization of how much has really changed.

I love it when clients leave my office committed to change and practice these principles. Almost always, they come back a few weeks later with a smile where there was once frustration, sadness, anger, or disappointment and are filled with joy and satisfaction. So many of us think everything would be great if other people changed, but in reality, other people become great when we are the ones who change. The world becomes a better place. This is the power of self-hypnosis.

It was 37 years ago that I was given a self-hypnosis relaxation cassette tape to listen to. I remember how when I first listened to the tape it sounded odd but was so calming. I came from a turbulent family, (you can listen to what I shared in my TEDx talk about this at SelfHypnosisSolution.com) and the experience created by that cassette set in motion a craving to understand the real power of self-hypnosis. My academic studies in counseling led me to understand deeper value in the resource state of self-hypnosis.

Although life has been far from perfect for me, it has been in the most difficult times that I have applied these techniques and created a way out from self-defeating patterns of behavior. With self-hypnosis I overcame a fear of flying, anxiousness about driving, stopped smoking, and learned to tame anxiety. More importantly though, I learned how to be patient with others, to put some space between me and my emotions, and to live fully in the present moment. The most powerful promise of self-hypnosis that I have realized in my life is that I can set an intention to not just solve a problem but to rise above the stress of any situation and excel. As parent, I learned how to share abundance with my children and the processes of critical thinking and clarity self-hypnosis provides. As a friend, I have learned forgiveness and compassion, and I have experienced the financial success of stepping up my game and working to the best of my abilities in business.

At the beginning of this book I asked you to identify your intention. What did you hope to gain by reading this book and mastering these ideas? Without a doubt, what might have seemed like a lofty or even unobtainable goal at the beginning of this book now has been accomplished or is at least within your sights.

Congratulations for learning self-hypnosis! It will be a life changer for you, and the promise of self-hypnosis is already being realized within you now.

Get the FREE Resources

That Come with This Book.

Make Sure You Access Them Here:

SelfHypnosisSolution.com

If you do not already have this book:

The Seven Most Effective Methods of Self-Hypnosis:
How to Create Rapid Change in Your Health,
Your Wealth, and Your Habits

Order it today from your favorite retailer!

**Please leave a 5-Star Review for This Book at the
retailer's webpage where you purchased this book!**

Made in United States
North Haven, CT
17 February 2024